Moral Principles and Social Values

Jennifer Trusted

ROUTLEDGE & KEGAN PAUL

London

First published in 1987 by
Routledge & Kegan Paul Ltd
11 New Fetter Lane, London EC4P 4EE

Set in Times, 10 on 12pt
by Inforum Ltd, Portsmouth
and printed in Great Britain
by TJ Press (Padstow) Ltd,
Padstow, Cornwall

British Library Cataloguing in Publication Data

Trusted, Jennifer
Moral principles and social values.
1. Ethics
I. Title
170   BJ1012

ISBN 0–7102–1047–7

Moral Principles and Social Values

The Author

Jennifer Trusted is part-time lecturer in philosophy at the University of Exeter Extra-Mural Department, and Tutor for the Open University 'Science and Belief' course. She is the author of *The Logic of Scientific Inference* (Macmillan, 1979), *An Introduction to the Philosophy of Knowledge* (Macmillan, 1981), *Free Will and Responsibility* (Oxford University Press, 1984) and *Inquiry and Understanding* (Macmillan, forthcoming).

CONTENTS

ACKNOWLEDGMENTS

I should like to thank Professor Sir Alfred Ayer for constructive criticism, especially in relation to chapter IV. I should also like to thank Mr Martin Davies for many helpful suggestions in relation to clarity and style and for the material from Hibbert quoted in chapter VIII.

INTRODUCTION

This book is written as an introduction to ethics for the educated reader who has no prior knowledge of the subject as a branch of philosophy. I also hope that it may serve as a textbook for philosophy students in sixth forms and starting at universities, and that it may prove useful to students in departments of law, politics, sociology and education. There are three principal aims: firstly to give an account of philosophical approaches to ethics, secondly to support the view that there are some basic moral principles that are universally acknowledged, and thirdly to show that ethics is a practical subject which affects our moral assessment of interpersonal behaviour and the conduct of public affairs.

The first six chapters of the book provide an outline of the nature of ethics and of ethical theories. I hope it will be useful to philosophy students as a résumé or as an introduction, and that it will provide an adequate base for the philosophical analysis of moral judgments for students in other fields and for the general reader. No prior knowledge is assumed and technical terms are at a minimum. When introduced they are explained in the text or in the glossary; if in the latter their first appearance is with an asterisk. The chapter headings indicate the scope of the text: there is a brief account of the nature of ethics and of the character of value judgments as compared with other judgments, then the interdependence of fact and value is discussed and the four main views of value judgments, emotivist, prescriptivist, consequentialist and intuitionist, are introduced. The treatment is historical so that a background to present-day opinions is provided. There is reference back to these first chapters throughout the text in order to stress how philosophical analysis clarifies issues in moral debate.

Our capacity for moral evaluation is taken as being self-evident; save for a relatively tiny number of psychopaths, adult human beings who are capable of reasoning at all have a moral sense and can make moral judgments. This is a contingent fact about human beings (we might have been different) but it *is* a fact, and therefore our concept of a human person is of a being who understands and values moral worth. It does not, of course, follow that people always behave as they think they ought to behave, or even that they always know *how* they ought to behave, for egotism and a limited power to solve moral problems are also universal human attributes. But though we do not expect moral perfection and moral omniscience we do expect moral awareness. In chapter VI (Intuitionism) I suggest that we all recognise and acknowledge two basic principles: keeping trust and benevolence. I argue, on the lines of Peter Singer, that our respect for these principles may well have evolved, so that our moral sense has a pragmatic basis in that a species valuing trust and showing benevolence will give its young a better chance to survive and reproduce than a species whose members are egotistical. I further suggest that just as other faculties, such as our power to reason logically and to calculate mathematically, have transcended the original pragmatic function, so our capacity to make moral assessments has transcended its original function of promoting group cohesion and protecting the young.

In the middle chapters I suggest that the view that there are no universally accepted moral principles arises because in different societies the concrete expectations as to how people *ought* to behave vary enormously. Thus though the principle of keeping trust and the principle of benevolence are basic everywhere, people of different cultures deem different conduct moral and immoral. In any given society what is expected and approved is explicitly or implicitly supported by secondary principles, derived from the basic principles; it is these secondary principles that are the basis of the social values and of the ground rules that characterise the society. Each individual's innate moral sense develops as she observes the way people behave in the society in which she grows up; each individual realises that she is expected to follow certain moral rules and conform to certain codes of behaviour. Most people come to relate the rules they learn as children to their society's secondary principles and social values but in general they do not appreciate that these are themselves supported (or are believed to be supported) by more fundamental principles. Hence they do not appreciate that there is a basic morality common to all societies.

Moral conflicts can arise. Some may be pseudo-moral conflicts in that they are largely debates about matters of fact, but others, genuine moral conflicts, involve genuine moral disagreement. There may be clashes of secondary principles within or between groups, and in such cases rational argument about the relation of these principles to the universally acknowledged primary principles is possible. Deeper conflicts involve clashes of the basic principles and in this case, though debate need not be entirely about feelings, there is an inevitable subjective element in proposed resolutions. Moral conflict is discussed in chapter IX.

Morality must be a social concept since it is concerned with our dealings with others, and in the last chapters (XI–XIII) issues related to public affairs are discussed. But throughout the text examples of current concerns are debated with reference to other authors, to letters written to the press and to the treatment of moral issues in literature. In addition the role of religion in morality is considered though whether it is a contingent fact that morality and religion are associated or whether the human moral sense cannot develop beyond the pragmatic and prudential without a religious background is left an open question.

It is inevitable that various aspects of moral judgments are repeated in different chapters. I do not think that this is a drawback for it helps readers to appreciate the various factors, moral, factual and social, that influence ethical situations. As far as possible I have cross-referenced themes in the text. There are some suggestions for reading which I hope will help those wishing to study further.

I

MORALITY DOES MATTER

Human beings can be morally evaluated as responsible agents who are free to choose how to act. Elsewhere[1] I have argued that our concept of a person is a concept of an individual with inner thoughts and feelings controlling his or her actions. I also suggested that an appreciation of moral values and the desire to act in accordance with those values can transcend the desire for survival[2] and that the view that we are, at least to some extent and in some situations, free agents is supported by the fact that human beings are moral agents. We all have moral values and we all make moral judgments.

To discuss moral values and moral judgments, that is to study ethics, is not to moralise; for in studying ethics we are concerned with the *nature* of moral judgments, not with making those judgments. If I say 'It is wrong to steal' to myself and/or to others I am moralising, but if I am concerned with the significance and import of the judgment 'It is wrong to steal' I am concerned with the judgment itself, not with the behaviour it condemns. Thus ethics is one remove from first-order morality. The kind of problems facing ethics can be appreciated by considering the types of questions asked about moral judgments. They are:

(1) Are moral judgments, such as 'It is wrong to steal', justified by appeal to fundamental and objective moral principles, or by appeal to social conventions, or are they merely subjective statements of personal opinion?

(2) Are they justified by an appeal to actual or probable or presumed consequences for human well-being?

(3) Are they not statements at all but either mere expressions of feeling, or expressions that also serve as guides to action?

(4) To what extent are moral judgments affected by factual circumstances, both particular and general, including our scientific knowledge of the world?
(5) Are they dependent on religious beliefs and does religion affect
personal and social morality?
(6) Can there be any universal moral judgments, valid for all moral
creatures in all places and at all times?
(7) To what extent are moral values affected by the society in which
we live, and by our family and cultural upbringing?

Some of these questions are closely related, for example (1), (5)
and (7), and they all need to be expanded in order to be answered.
But they give some idea of the subject matter of ethics, and also of
its complexity and its importance. Ethics is not only of theoretical
importance, because the answers we give to ethical questions will
profoundly affect our view of first-order morality. The way we
decide to assess, for example, 'It is wrong to steal' will affect our
own behaviour and also our attitude to the behaviour of others; it
will also affect our views about social conventions and laws.

It is unlikely that human beings will agree in their assessments of
moral judgments, for moral behaviour cannot be completely independent of empirical* circumstances and so cannot be simply and
neatly related to principles. But by seeking answers to ethical
questions we may hope to reveal some basic moral values and principles and to see how they give support to moral judgments. In
addition we may hope to assess the role that human needs and
desires play in moral (and immoral) behaviour, and to assess the
role of reason in the making of moral judgments. All this should
contribute to reducing thoughtless judgments made without consideration of relevant factors and so we should be better placed to
make sound moral judgments on practical issues involving personal
morality and social policy. Thus ethics, second-order morality, will
affect first-order morality and moralising and, indirectly, will help
in the making of sensible and constructive proposals as to what
should be done. Writing of moral philosophy (ethics), David
Raphael says:

> Most people do not study the subject simply for the fun of it.
> The inquiry arises from a problem of real life. If I have come to
> doubt moral beliefs which I previously took for granted, and if I
> therefore ask whether there are good reasons for or against

acceptance, I seriously want to know what I should believe about right and wrong. To ask, in the face of the conflicting codes of conduct, whether there is good reason to accept one and reject the rest, is virtually to ask which, if any, is really right. If we succeeded in showing that one was really right, that would come pretty close to showing how we ought to behave.[3]

Aristotle called ethics 'practical reason', and he distinguished it from 'speculative reason'. The latter consisted of logic, metaphysics and natural philosophy (today called 'science' or 'natural science'). In common with medieval Christian theologians and philosophers, Aristotle regarded practical reason as being far more important than speculative reason because it was concerned with how we behaved. As John Finnis says, 'By "practical" . . . I do not mean "workable" as opposed to unworkable, efficient as opposed to inefficient; I mean "with a view to decision and action". Practical thought is thinking about what (one ought) to do.'[4] Aristotle thought that by applying themselves to practical reasons people could acquire deeper understanding of moral judgments and moral values and therefore would know that the best human life was one lived in accord with moral principles. Any person who understood the nature of morality would know that right conduct was a necessary condition for self-fulfillment, *arete*.[5] His *Ethics* opens with: 'Every art and every investigation and similarly every action and pursuit, is aimed at some good. Hence the Good has been rightly defined as "that at which all things aim".'[6]

One objection to this account of the Good is that human nature appears to be over-rated; it is obvious that not everyone wants to act for the Good, and not everyone aims for the Good. Aristotle would have granted that relatively few people aim for the Good for he was aware that relatively few people are wise and know what is the best way to live. It is the wise who know that to act morally is to fulfil the aspirations of human nature; this knowledge is, indeed, what makes them wise. Aristotle believed, as did Socrates and Plato before him, and as did the Christian theologians who followed him, that not to act for the Good was a mark of ignorance and folly. It was, therefore, irrational to choose to act wrongly (immorally) for it was only by acting rightly (morally) that it was possible to achieve what *must* be every person's ultimate desire.

Another objection to Aristotle's account of the Good is that he has produced a circular definition: All actions and pursuits are aimed at some good, hence the Good is that at which all things aim. This does not tell us what the Good *is*; the second statement appears merely to repeat the first. It seems that Aristotle thought that we all had an intuitive notion of the Good, and his opening sentences are to be regarded rather as a means of stressing the relation between our intuitive knowledge and action, rather than as a definition of the Good *per se*. How far knowledge of the Good *is* a matter of intuition, and whether intuition does give grounds for asserting that some person or action is good, will be a major concern of any book on ethics.

Christian theologians, such as St Thomas Aquinas, held that the ultimate aim of all human beings must be to contemplate the beatific vision of God in heaven, and to achieve this a person had to be in a state of grace. Adam and Eve had fallen from their natural state of grace when they ate the fruit of the Tree of Knowledge in the Garden of Eden,[7] but in so doing they acquired knowlege of good and evil and the power to make moral judgments. All mankind had inherited this power, which Aquinas called *synderesis*: through synderesis, and with God's help and Christ's sacrifice, all could regain the state of grace lost at the Fall.

Both the Greek view of virtue as an essential part of a full life and self-fulfilment, and the Christian view of virtue as required for a state of grace, a state necessary for deserving eternal bliss in paradise, affect our concept of virtue and morality today[8] whether or not we have read the classics and whether or not we are Christian believers. But, as described, the concept is far too crude, and would have been regarded as crude by the Ancient Greeks and by Christian thinkers. It is too crude because it appears to commend virtue as a matter of policy: the policy of being virtuous so as to achieve self-fulfilment on earth or eternal bliss in a life to come. Most of us do not regard virtue as being dependent on policy; we do not think that moral behaviour is simply politic behaviour. We would agree with Archbishop Whately's apopthegm: 'Honesty is the best policy; but he who is governed by that maxim is not an honest man.'[9]

The force of the apopthegm comes from our belief that an honest man is not honest as a matter of *policy*; he is honest because he wants to *be* honest. The phrase 'best policy' customarily means 'better for one's own interests' or 'better for the interest of one's particular clique', because it furthers either short-term or long-term

4

desires. To act with enlightened self-interest is to further long-term, as opposed to short term, desires. But any form of self- or own-group-interest does not give a motive for truly moral behaviour; at best the most is amoral. It would be in a person's interest to give up smoking, for smoking is likely to harm health, but such a policy of self-denial would be for prudential, not moral reasons. Likewise a policy to eat less in order to have a slim figure or to keep healthy is prudential; again it is amoral. Other prudential policies can be immoral; for example to adopt a policy of consistent honesty so as to build up a reputation of trustworthiness such that it would become possible to obtain a large sum of money by fraud and not be suspected, or to decide to be kind and attentive to an elderly person in order to gain a large bequest at the expense of relatives. The point is that self-interest, whether long-term or short-term, whether amoral or immoral, carries a notion of personal (or clique) gain: better health, better looks, more material goods, increased power, higher status, and so on. If we take the phrase 'best policy' to mean not just 'better for one's own interests' but *also* 'achievement of moral worth' we are using 'best policy' in an ambiguous and unusual way. If 'best policy' can mean 'increase in moral worth' then the Archbishop's apophthegm loses its force and indeed ceases to be acceptable for it would then be possible to interpret it as: 'Honesty is the achievement of moral worth, but he who is governed by that maxim is not an honest man.'

If we act virtuously purely because we respect virtue and want to be decent people, we are not motivated by 'policy' in its usual and pejorative sense. We are not acting out of self-interest, as self-interest is generally understood; rather we are acting with the interests of others in mind – and not just associates or members of a particular clique – we want to adhere to principles of conduct that we deem to be morally right. Thus the prime motive is the wish to be moral, and virtue is the only desired reward; it does not degrade a virtuous action, and transform it into 'policy', to affirm that the agent's motive was to *be* virtuous. Those who act virtuously for this reason are virtuous, but those who decide to act virtuously as a matter of policy are not. Furthermore the latter are unlikely to continue to act virtuously, for their attitude entails that if the virtuous action will not promote self-interest it will be abandoned. Shakespeare lets Falstaff express the view of those who do not value a virtue for its own sake:

. . . honour pricks me on. Yea, but how if honour pricks me off
when I come on? how then? Can honour set a leg? no: or an
arm? no: or take away the grief of a wound? no. Honour hath no
skill in surgery then? no. What is honour? a word. What is in
that word honour? what is that honour? air. A trim reckoning!
who hath it? he that died o'Wednesday. Doth he feel it? no.
Doth he hear it? no. 'Tis insensible, then? yea, to the dead. But
will it not live with the living? no. Why? detraction will not
suffer it. Therefore I'll none of it. Honour is a mere scutcheon:
and so ends my catechism.[10]

Few people in Shakespeare's time, in our own time, or at any time,
would accept Falstaff's view.[11] Morality matters and such words as
'honour', 'trust' and 'kindness' are not mere sounds or marks on
paper; nor are they guides to promoting self-interest. What then
gives moral judgments their force? *Why* does morality matter?

II

JUDGMENTS

Judgments are verbally embodied in statements, sentences that assert that something is or is not the case and can therefore be true or false. Statements[1] are to be distinguished from other kinds of sentences, such as questions ('How are you today?'), commands and requests ('No smoking' and 'Please shut the door'), exclamations ('O for the wings of a dove!') and subjunctives ('She might arrive today'). All these sentences make sense and are useful, but they do not make assertions and so they are not judgments. As we shall see there are different kinds of judgments; moral (and aesthetic) judgments are commonly called *value judgments*. There are diverse opinions as to the nature of value judgments and many philosophers would deny that value judgments are genuine judgments, in that they would deny that judgments of moral (and aesthetic) content are assertions. These opinions will be discussed but, to start with, we shall take sentences concerned with moral behaviour as judgments and distinguish four types of judgment:[2] logical/mathematical, empirical, metaphysical and value judgments.

LOGICAL/MATHEMATICAL JUDGMENTS

Examples are: 'If A is greater than B, and B is greater than C, then A is greater than C' and '2 + 2 = 4'.

The distinctive feature of these judgments is that they are judged to be true or false primarily through reason. It does not follow that we do not appeal to observation in order to understand them by, for example, drawing diagrams or counting beans, but once we have understood such a judgment, we appreciate that it is known to be true (or false) by the exercise of reason. We all acknowledge this; the comedy in the following passage arises on that account. It is from Eugene Ionescu's play *The Lesson:*

PROFESSOR   That's just the way things are, Mademoiselle, it can't be explained. You understand it by a sort of mathematical sense inside you. Either you've got it or you haven't.

PUPIL: There's nothing can help me then!

PROFESSOR   Listen, Mademoiselle! If you don't succeed in fully understanding these archetypal arithmetical principles, you'll never succeed in carrying out your work properly as a polytechnician . . . if you've not mastered these elementary propositions, how can you ever hope to make mental calculations . . . such as this, for example: how much is three billion, seven hundred and fifty-five million, nine hundred and ninety-eight thousand, two hundred and fifty one, multiplied by five billion, one hundred and sixty-two million, three hundred and three thousand, five hundred and eight?

PUPIL: (*very rapidly*) That makes nineteen quillion, three hundred and ninety quadrillion, two trillion, eight hundred and forty-four billion, two hundred and nineteen million, a hundred and sixty-four thousand, five hundred and eight. . .

PROFESSOR   . . . Yes . . . you're right, by Jove. . . But how did you arrive at that, if you don't understand the principles of arithmetical calculation?

PUPIL: Oh! It's quite easy, really! As I can't depend on reasoning it out I learnt off by heart all the possible combinations in multiplication.

PROFESSOR: But the combinations are infinite!

PUPIL: I managed to do it, anyway!

PROFESSOR   It's quite astounding!   Nevertheless, you will allow me to point out to you that I am by no means satisfied. . . . You ought to have found the answer

8

by a dual process of inductive and deductive mathematical reasoning, and that is the way you should have arrived at all your answers.[3]

The comedy of the situation is a consequence of our knowledge that mathematical problems are *not* solved by appeals to knowledge of past particular instances; solutions do not depend on memory of facts, but on the understanding and application of mathematical principles, we may say of the conventions of mathematics. Our quotation shows that aspect of mathematical reasoning: 'You understand it by a sort of mathematical sense inside you.' We do not regard this statement as mysterious, as describing some arcane feature of human abilities. It is simply a matter of fact that most people, if taught to apply the principles when at school, just do understand simple mathematical reasoning and can use the symbols and techniques.

Even though the faculty by which we reason is a personal capacity for each individual, the answers to simple mathematical problems are regarded as objectively right (or wrong). This is because, given any simple problem, there will be general agreement as to what the answer is and what are valid ways of arriving at that answer. The objectivity is a consequence of the plain fact that most human beings show themselves able to reason mathematically and do reason in the same way; thus there is inter-subjective agreement about the solutions of problems and about how these solutions are found.[4]

EMPIRICAL JUDGMENTS

Examples are: 'Water is essential for life' and 'That water is hot'.

The distinctive feature of these judgments is that they are taken to be true (or false) primarily by appeal to what is observed. We need to reason in order to interpret the deliverances of our senses, but without sense-perception there could be no empirical judgments. There are two kinds of empirical judgments: there are judgments of an individual's sense experiences and there are judgments that purport to give descriptions of the world that are not dependent on the experiences of any particular individual. Examples of the former are given by Nowell-Smith:

Direct observation often gives different results when there is no reason to suppose that the object observed has changed. The suitcase that felt light when I left the station feels heavy after I have walked a mile; yet no one has put anything in it. In one of the standard examples of optical illusion a certain line appears curved but when a rule is put against it it appears to be straight; yet no one has altered the position of the ink on the paper. A piece of paper that looked white before looks red under a red light.[5]

As Nowell-Smith says, we have two languages, in that we have two ways of presenting empirical accounts. One language is used to describe sense experiences (subjective sensations) and the other language describes how we think things really are; this is the language describing what we take as objective empirical facts. Now, superficially at least, this dichotomy is paradoxical for any empirical knowledge must be supported by evidence provided by perception of how things seem to individuals. Nowell-Smith illustrates the difference between how things *seem* and how they *are*, and highlights the paradox:

> Now it is an essential feature of the double language of 'looks or feels' and 'really is' that, while the observer is allowed to be the best judge of how a thing looks or feels to him, he is not allowed to be the best judge of what it really is. If two cakes feel equally heavy to me but the balance shows one to be heavier than the other, I must say that one of them was really heavier all the time; but I am not compelled to say that it must have *felt* heavier. Obviously it did not. . . .
>
> The double language enables me to deal with this sort of situation. 'They both *felt* the same to me', I shall say, 'but one of them must really have *been* heavier all along.'[6]

The resolution of the paradox, that is showing *how* it is possible to make objective judgments on the basis of subjective sense experience, depends on the contingent fact that it just happens to be the case that we can usually find a way of describing observable features of the world (for example, the weight of cakes) in a way that commands universal assent, e.g. by reference to the reading of a pointer against a scale. It is this universal assent which makes it possible to have objective facts and to speak in the language of the way things *are*, rather than the language of the way things seem.

For example, we can say that a surface is really white, in an objective sense, because it happens to be the case that every observer agrees that it is white when viewed in daylight and we stipulate that the real colour of any surface is the colour it seems to be when viewed by a normally sighted observer in daylight.[7] Thus we bridge the gap between the way things seem to people and the way things really are.[8] There is no contradiction in 'This paper is really white but it looks red now' because we are using the word 'white' as a word from the objective language and the word 'red' as a word from the subjective language. The sentence is equivalent to 'This paper looks white to all normally sighted observers when viewed in daylight but it looks red to me in the present circumstances'.

It is not always possible to get inter-subjective agreement, and therefore objective judgments, by simple inspection, even under standard conditions, such as daylight for assessing colour. For centuries, judgments of the temperature of objects were both vague and subjective because the only way of estimating temperature was by its effect on an individual's skin.[9] According to circumstances, different people would make different assessments; indeed the same person could arrive at conflicting assessments. For example, if we have a bowl of hot water, a bowl of icy water and a bowl of tepid water, then, if one hand is put in the hot water, the other in the icy water and afterwards both hands are put in the tepid water, we find that judging by the effect on the hand that has been in the hot water, we would take the tepid water to be cold, but judging by the effect on the hand that has been in the icy water, we would take the tepid water to be hot.

Today we still make rough estimates of temperature using our subjective reactions – the elbow in the baby's bath, the hot iron held close to the face – but we are aware that there is a considerable element of subjectivity in such methods and we rely on thermometers to give objective assessments, that is the *real* temperature. The thermometer reading is objective because it happens to be the case that thermometer readings, like all readings depending on matching a pointer on a scale, command universal agreement. Words like 'hot' and 'cold' may, therefore, be given an objective sense by stipulative definition. We may stipulate that water above 40°C is hot because most people, on most occasions, do experience a sensation of hotness from water at that temperature. Having defined 'hot' objectively it is not contradictory to say 'This water is not really hot but it feels hot to me'. The same word, 'hot', is being used firstly in the objective language and secondly in the subjective language. The sentence is equivalent to 'This water is not at 40°C but it feels hot to me just now'.

So we can make objective empirical judgments,[10] but it is worth stressing that it just happens to be the case that we can, generally, devise methods that command agreement. Just as we can all come to the same conclusions when we reason logically or mathematically,[11] so we can make the same inferences from suitably chosen sense experiences. Nowell-Smith points out that general agreement does not in itself show that our judgments are correct, but, though not a sufficient* condition for objective judgments it is a necessary* condition for them:

> I am not arguing that general agreement is a conclusive test of the presence or degree of a real property. Our ordinary objective language makes truth independent of opinion and allows for the possibility, however remote, of everybody being mistaken. A Gallup Poll could not settle the question whether the earth is round. General agreement is not a test of truth; but is a necessary condition of the use of objective language.[12]

There have been philosophers of science[13] who have argued that the sophisticated empirical knowledge we call scientific knowledge is not objective in an *absolute* sense since it depends on the implicit acceptance of paradigm theories that may come to be rejected later. For example, the Ptolemaic astronomical paradigm that placed the earth at the centre of the universe provided a means of interpreting observations made on the heavenly bodies. During the time that the paradigm theory was accepted it was an objective fact that the earth was at rest and that the sun, and indeed all the heavenly bodies, revolved round it. Today our Copernican paradigm leads us to take the daily revolution of the earth and its annual circuit round the sun as objective facts.

There is no general agreement as to the epistemological* status of scientific theories, but even those who regard the acceptance of a paradigm as being largely dependent on non-rational influences, such as cultural conditioning and individual psychological prejudices, would hesitate to say that scientific knowledge is not

12

objective knowledge. At the very least it is objective within the framework of a paradigm and many philosophers of science would claim that we are justified in regarding science as a search for objective truth[14] even though we may never be certain that truth has been attained. But in any case it is generally accepted that common-sense empirical judgments and scientific judgments can be objective judgments in the sense that we expect there to be inter-subjective agreement. If such a view is queried by the sceptic we are entitled to ask her whether *any* judgment can be objective and, if not, how she distinguishes what are commonly taken as objective statements – matters of empirical fact and mathematical theorems – from descriptions and expressions of personal feelings, opinions and beliefs. When we consider the degree of objectivity of other kinds of judgments – rational, metaphysical and evaluative – we tend to take the empirical judgments of science and mathematics as exemplars of what an objective judgment is.

METAPHYSICAL JUDGMENTS

Examples are: 'We have free will and not all our actions are physically determined' and 'Space is indefinitely extended'.

The distinctive feature of these judgments is that they make assertions about the nature of the world yet they cannot be estab-lished as true or false by appeal to sense perception. On account of this some philosophers would prefer to call them beliefs rather than judgments. They consider it clearer to reserve the term 'judgment' for statements that can be shown to be true or false by appeal to ratiocination or observation. However, metaphysical judgments are assertions and here they will be treated as a kind of judgment.

Metaphysical judgments cannot be established as true or false by observation because they transcend or 'go beyond' the ordinary empirical judgments of common sense and science, and they pro-vide the 'rules' for logical thought. They can be regarded as giving us the framework within which we can make empirical and logical judgments. They cannot be *proved* but it has been argued that they are self-evident in the way that moral principles are self-evident.

. . . what is certain is that the natural sciences and in general all theoretical disciplines rest implicitly on epistemic* principles, or

13

norms of theoretical rationality which are undemonstrated, indemonstrable, but self-evident in a manner strongly analogous to the self-evidence ascribed by Aquinas to the basic principles of practical reasonableness.[15]

Finnis stresses the particular importance of logic:

> . . . the natural sciences (not to mention the historical sciences, and the disciplined common sense of forensic assessment of evidence) certainly rest, implicitly but thoroughly, on the principles of elementary formal logic[16]

and those principles are themselves to be accepted without proof:

> These norms or principles of theoretical rationality underpin all our thinking . . . it is, in short, a principle of theoretical rationality that one ought to accept deductive arguments that seem valid, even though no justification of the inference is possible.[17]

The only support that metaphysical judgments get and can get is analogous to the support for paradigm theories (see above) in that they should allow us to make consistent explanations of our experiences. In so far as they do this we regard them as reliable. Not that we normally question *basic* metaphysical judgments; in this respect they are very different from paradigm scientific theories. Unlike the latter, basic metaphysical judgments arise intuitively and, commonly, are never assessed but simply taken for granted as self-evident truths. For example, we intuitively 'place' objects and events in a three-dimensional Euclidean space[18] which extends indefinitely in all directions. We do not normally reflect or deliberate about this judgment; it is a basic assumption that gives us a way of spontaneously interpreting our sense experiences. Similarly we intuitively assume that other people have thoughts and feelings like our own and that they are free agents, responsible, at least to some extent, for what they do. Again we do not reflect on this intuition, it helps us to understand the way others behave and it is part of our concept of a person. The concept embraces the assumption that persons are moral agents, aware of what it is to act rightly (and wrongly) in the moral sense of 'right' and 'wrong'.

Fundamental and intuitive metaphysical judgments are not sacrosanct; they may come to be modified. Thus though we spon-

14

taneously take space to be Euclidean space,[19] science now tells us that, strictly speaking, this is not the case, The scientific arguments show that sophisticated empirical enquiry yields other evidence that makes it necessary for us to alter our intuitive concepts about the nature of the world if we are to have a consistent and coherent explanation of our experiences. Nevertheless, we still interpret our visual and other sense experiences so as to 'place' physical objects in an indefinitely extended three-dimensional (though not quite Euclidean) space, even in scientific accounts. Our metaphysical judgments cannot be *derived* from other judgments but this does not mean that they cannot be objective. As Finnis says:

> in every field there is and must be, at some point or points, an end to derivation and inference. At that point or points we will find ourselves in face of the self-evident, which makes possible all subsequent inferences in that field.[20]

The metaphysical judgment 'There is free will' which is undoubtedly the judgment we make spontaneously has been rejected by some philosophers. They hold that if there is to be a consistent account of cause and effect in the world the view of persons as agents, independent of, or rather not completely dependent on, physical events must be rejected. Those who disagree consider that the concept of a person as an agent is one that has to be retained and that our concept of causality must be modified. I have argued elsewhere[21] that there can be no appeal to facts to decide this issue. For our metaphysical beliefs underpin the relevant facts.

In the 1920s and 1930s logical positivists such as A.J. Ayer argued that metaphysics was meaningless and that metaphysical judgments were empty of content because they could not be established as true (or false) by perception or by reason. But we cannot dispense with metaphysics; we have to assent to some metaphysical beliefs and judgments. There is no doubt that the metaphysical judgments that command universal assent ('There are objects in a three-dimensional space', for example, or 'Other people have thoughts and feelings like our own') are taken as objective judgments. No one seriously questions the objectivity of the judgment that space is three-dimensional and is indefinitely extended, that there are causal relations between events and that there are objects existing independently of any person (or animal) perceiving them. Even when a metaphysical judgment does not command universal assent, for example 'All human actions are determined by physical laws', it is not necessarily held to be irredeemably subjective.

VALUE JUDGMENTS

Examples are: 'It is wrong to tell a lie' and 'It is better to give than to receive'.

The distinctive feature of these judgments is that they are evaluations against a standard that is acknowledged by the person making the judgment; if the judgment is to be taken as an objective judgment, the standard must command universal assent (as do objective logical and empirical judgments) or it must command substantial agreement (as do some objective metaphysical judgments). The two examples given are moral evaluations. There are also aesthetic value judgments, for example, 'No picture should have a large area of blue' and 'Mozart was a great composer'. But we are primarily concerned with moral value judgments and shall refer to aesthetic judgments only when they may help to illuminate issues arising in the study of moral judgments.

Philosophers have taken different views as to the nature of value judgments; as we shall see some have thought that they are not really judgments at all and so cannot be said to be true or false. But all would agree that whatever their status, evaluations often refer to and appeal implicitly to facts, and that many incorporate factual descriptions. Moreover it is generally not possible to make a firm distinction between factual (or allegedly factual) descriptions and evaluations. We shall consider the interdependence of fact and value in the next chapter.

III

FACT AND VALUE

The majority of descriptions of human activities contain explicit or implicit evaluations. Overt evaluations lie in all directly evaluative words and in words used in an evaluative sense; less obvious evaluations depend on context. Take what can be a purely factual description: 'She arrived at nine o'clock.' Now if those who heard or read this had been aware that 'she' had been expected at half past eight the phrase would carry disapprobation; it would carry even stronger disapprobation if it were known that she had *promised* to arrive at half past eight. Thus, though none of the words are even partly evaluative, the context can make the description evaluative.

If evaluative words are used the evaluation is less dependent on contextual knowledge. Thus 'She arrived on time' and 'She arrived late' are evaluative in a plainer way than 'She arrived at nine o'clock'. Yet the first two sentences tell us less about the time of arrival than does the last; so though they give us a more definite evaluation they give less specific factual information. We may find the evaluation more helpful than the fact about the time but it is worth noting that evaluations can avoid reference to factual detail even though knowledge of the factual detail might affect the evaluation! For example 'She arrived late' might be said of someone arriving just one minute after the expected time or one hour after, and the degree of disapprobation would almost certainly be different. The word 'late' is semi-evaluative for it does not carry moral disapprobation invariably; by contrast words like 'betray', 'kindly' and 'faithful' are unequivocally evaluative. It follows that simple judgments, such as 'It is wrong to betray', 'It is good to be kind' and 'We ought to keep faith', are pleonastic in that the evaluative words already carry the moral judgment.

17

A common mistake in moral discussion is to use value-loaded words as though they were value-neutral. Thus a conscientious objector may argue against war on the grounds that murder is wrong. But by using the word 'murder' she has effectively begged the question; the discussion must then be concerned not with whether murder is wrong but whether killing people in war *is* murder, in the accepted sense of 'murder'. Of course the conscientious objector believes that it is but it is up to her to give *reasons* for this belief. Then we will get a clearer and more profitable ethical discussion. Bearing this in mind consider the judgment said to have been made by E.M. Forster: 'If I had to betray my country or my friend I hope I should have the guts to betray my country.' It embodies a number of implicit value judgments:

(a) It is wrong to betray one's country.
(b) It is wrong to betray one's friends.
(c) It is a greater wrong to betray the trust of a friend than to betray one's country.
(d) It is courageous to act as one thinks is right if this involves opposing the laws of one's country and, very probably, also opposing the general public opinion.

From the discussion above we can see that the first two judgments, (a) and (b), are tautologous.[1] The last judgment, (d), is also indisputable for it must be courageous to do what one thinks is right and thereby risk punishment and censure. We may feel that the courage is misplaced in that we do not agree that the action *is* right; but we cannot deny that courage is shown. Judgment (c) is the most perplexing and the most interesting because the assertion implies that there is one (morally) best way to resolve a moral conflict.

In discussing (c) we should note that in this context both the words 'country' and 'friend' are evaluative in that they carry implications of a special duty of trust. There are other cases of special obligation: of parents to children and vice versa, of doctors to patients, of priests to their flock. British law forbids forcing a wife to give evidence against her husband and *vice versa*, and though other relationships, such as parent and child, are not legally protected, individuals may be admired if they refuse to comply with the law and betray confidences. Our society rates certain types of trust higher than others but there are areas in dispute; for example some people would have journalists protected so that they are not required to reveal their sources of information to a court, just as solicitors and barristers cannot be required to reveal confidential communications with their clients. Most people think that it is better *not* to force doctors and priests to divulge confidential information because the long-term effects of betrayal would produce more harm than that caused by actual or potential criminals being at large. There is no general agreement as to whether it is in the public interest for journalists to be similarly protected.[2] The law is primarily concerned with social consequences rather than with personal morality, but individuals may take the issue to be primarily a matter of moral principle.

By putting forward his moral judgments in a deliberately provocative form, Forster shows that he recognises that trusts and duties can be in moral conflict. One outstanding feature of (c) is that few would want to express agreement or disagreement without knowing more about the facts of the case. We need to know about the friend and his or her motives; we need to know more about the country and its government; we need to know the nature of the betrayal, that is *how* the country will be betrayed if trust is kept with the friend. It is therefore impossible to assent to or to deny the general judgment 'It is a greater wrong to betray the trust of a friend than to betray one's country'. Forster, as we shall see below, made his remark with particular circumstances in mind; but let us consider a variety of circumstances that may profoundly affect our assessment of the judgment; sometimes we shall see there is no *moral* dilemma.

For example, say I am a German living in Nazi Germany or a Russian in Stalinist Russia and I have a friend who reveals that she is working (undercover) against the government, a government which I also detest. If I keep my trust with her, and thereby also help to undermine the government, I shall have no guilty conscience and no moral conflict. I could well argue that apart from my positive duty to my friend, I am acting in the interests of my country by conniving at the overthrow of the current government. Of course it will take courage, perhaps very great courage, not to betray my friend but I know that I *ought* not to betray her. Again, if I wholeheartedly support the government of my country and discover, to my sorrow, that a friend is working to overthrow it I am not faced with a moral dilemma. I know very well that I *ought* to betray my friend; it will perhaps require great determination because of my affection but, as before, I know what I *ought* to do. Thus, in circumstances similar to the first example, we assent to judgment (c) and in circumstances similar to the second example we reject it. In both cases it may be hard for us to act as we know we ought to act but there is no moral problem in either type of situation.

But consider a situation (and this is the situation envisaged by Forster) in which we have doubts, serious doubts, as to the justice of our own government and we discover that a friend is working for another nation which has a government that we believe to be more just. Where does our moral duty lie? Take, for example, the case of a liberal socialist living in Britain in the 1930s; she thinks that a capitalist society cannot, in its very nature, ever give the mass of people a fulfilling life, and that a fundamental change is highly desirable. All the same she believes that a change should come through the decisions of elected representatives in Parliament. Then she finds out that a friend is working to betray their country to a nation with a government that they both sincerely believe to be better able to give most of its citizens a fulfilling life – that is a nation with a better government than that of their own country. Here there is a moral dilemma: there is affection for the friend and an acknowledgment of a duty of trust, for the friend would not have revealed her secret to a stranger or to a casual acquaintance; and although the liberal does not completely agree with what her friend is doing, she has some sympathy. On the other hand she also has a sense of responsibility towards the people of her own country in that she knows most of them would not want to be betrayed to a foreign power, and be dominated by it, even though, in her view, there would be fairer and better government. There is also a respect for the democratic system whereby the country is governed and the belief that change ought (morally) to come through parliament. Hence there is a real moral dilemma because it is not clear what is the (morally) right thing to do. We see that Forster believed that the right action was to avoid betraying a friend. Taking the judgment in its 1930s context, we can appreciate the force of the dilemma and also that it would take courage not to betray the friend because discovery would entail social censure. Knowing what we know in the 1980s we may think that Forster's judgment was wrong, but this is not because moral outlooks have changed (or not necessarily for this reason) but because we assess the facts of the situation differently.

Events of the last fifty years have revealed new facts and they have altered our view of what would be the right thing to do. Our new appraisal also leads us to use different descriptions of the situation. In the 1930s we might have said that our friend was an *idealist* working for *social justice*; today we would be more inclined to say that she was *spying* so as to introduce *dictatorship*. So, because of a different view of the situation we give a very different evaluative account and the account itself mirrors the new facts. There is an interdependence of factual and evaluative description: facts alter evaluations and evaluations alter facts. This is to be expected for facts and values are both expressed in words and words that are descriptive (factual) very often have evaluative overtones; words that are primarily evaluative can have descriptive (factual) significance.

As we have seen, the evaluative force of words can alter with context and with background knowledge, though the more purely evaluative words do not vary so much in this way. Words such as 'good', 'right', 'bad' and 'wrong' are so purely evaluative that they are independent of context and they carry unequivocal moral approbation and disapprobation with them. They will, of course, be applied to different people and different situations by different people and at different times, depending on the moral conventions that are accepted. For example today (in Britain) we believe that it is wrong to burn people at the stake for religious reasons[3] although three hundred years ago it would have been thought right to do so; but though our attitude to the action has changed, the moral significance of the word 'wrong' remains constant.

At the other end of the evaluative/descriptive scale are words like 'nine o'clock' that are descriptive and only acquire value overtones in context; examples of value-neutral words are 'yellow', 'cubic', 'rocky' and 'distant'.[4] It is possible to construct sentences in which such words carry some evaluative force, but that force must be context-dependent. Thus 'She knew that I was going to wear my yellow dress' (and deliberately wore something to clash with it) or (and kindly avoided wearing something that would clash with it). Because any evaluation is heavily context-dependent these descriptive words may carry approval or disapproval, and to be aware of what the moral evaluation is we must be aware of the context.[5]

These are the extremes; many words are evaluative and descriptive; examples are 'timid', 'prudent', 'unadventurous', 'rash', 'courageous', 'traditional', 'revolutionary', 'reforming' and so on.

Some, like 'thrifty', tend to carry approbation and others, say 'parsimonious', tend to carry disapprobation; with yet others, say 'mean', the evaluative force is stronger. Now the very same individual might be described by any one of those terms and the description would carry mild approbation, mild disapprobation or stronger disapprobation with it. Our own views of a person will almost certainly affect our choice; we have the old joke 'I am firm; you are obstinate; he is pig-headed' and the same joke is in 'I am thrifty; you are parsimonious; she is mean'. It is because our choice of word cannot but be a choice of value that factual accounts tend to become evaluations even though no purely evaluative word, like 'right' or 'wrong', is used.

There are many words that have acquired evaluative overtones, though they might have originally been purely descriptive. Examples are 'black' (as applied to people's skin), 'Jewish', 'old', 'young', 'feminist' and 'middle-class'. The evaluative force, and even the nature of the evaluation – whether commendatory or dismissive – will depend on context; hence they can be used to imply praise or censure. These descriptive words acquire evaluative force because social and moral conventions change, and their evaluative impact depends on the accepted conventions. The examples given are of words that have become evaluative; there are also words, still in current use, that have lost evaluative force. Examples are 'chaste', 'philanderer' and 'atheist'. The word 'chaste' had a very strong commendatory evaluative force in the nineteenth century and earlier, particularly as applied to women. Without that virtue other virtues were of little account in making a moral judgment of a woman; with that virtue other moral defects were insignificant. Today, though chastity has approximately the same descriptive meaning, its evaluative force is much reduced because attitudes to sex, and attitudes to female enjoyment of sex, have changed. For the same reason 'philanderer' has lost its overtones of disapprobation – though these were never so strong as was 'promiscuous' when applied to women. Likewise changing attitudes to religious beliefs have removed the moral censure from 'atheist', though its descriptive meaning is unchanged.

There are also words that have a different descriptive meaning (and therefore a different evaluative significance) for different people living in the same society at the same time. The following letter from *The Times* shows that different understandings or concepts of hardship affect evaluative judgments of government policy; the writer is referring to a dispute about Health Service salaries:

> 'Sir, Mr Frank Chapple, no liar, is deluding himself when he says that everyone supports the health workers except Mr Fowler. It is just that few of Mr Fowler's supporters can be heard from inside a trade union headquarters. The case that we ought not to devalue the skill and so must not pay more to the lower-paid workers only, and that the price of a greater rise all round is more than the rest of us can afford, is almost inaudible from there.
>
> We must alleviate hardship, but hardship is children without shoes, Lowry people with too little to eat, damp walls and leaky ceilings. It is not involved in cutting out smoking, drinking, betting and holidaying abroad.
>
> Almost the only avoidable hardship after 35 years of reasonably good government affects two classes of people, those overlooked as individuals by imperfections in the administration and those who are robbed of what they are entitled to, such as the sick, by people who are trying to take more of the inessentials of life than they are able to obtain without menace.
>
> Yours faithfully, D.YOUNG, Scotland[6]

Not everyone will agree with the view of hardship expressed in this letter but this in itself helps to show how important it is to come to an understanding of the *descriptive* content of words before making moral evaluations. Any discussion about whether hardship ought or ought not to be relieved, and at what cost to others, is useless if the disputants have different concepts of hardship and have failed to appreciate that this is the case. In addition any explanation of the *existence* of hardship depends on the concept of hardship assumed by those who offer the explanation.

Evaluative/descriptive words, especially those with fluid moral and descriptive significance (fluid because they depend on context and on user), commonly confuse moral discourse and practical discourse. There are an indefinitely large number of examples: those given above (pages 21–2), and many others, such as 'trendy', 'snigger' and 'do-gooder'. We cannot avoid using words carrying evaluative overtones and words with fluid meanings, but we can take care to recognise the difficulties. It is only if they are recognised that sensible and potentially helpful discussion is possible. It is necessary to recognise, for example, that people talking of 'protecting the rights of minorities' may be referring to the same problem as those who talk of 'barricading sectional interests'; that those who talk of 'maintaining law and order' may refer to the same events as those who talk of 'police state', that people who talk of 'freedom of the individual' may talk of the same issue as those who talk of 'selfish interests', and so on.

In chapter II we saw that empirical descriptions could be in two languages: the subjective language of personal sense experiences and the objective language of facts. The two languages are possible (that is there can be an objective as well as a subjective language) because it has been found that there is a very high degree of interpersonal agreement in describing what we perceive. Common-sense qualitative observations can be made quantitative and precise by using instruments: rulers, clocks, thermometers, etc. These instruments are useful because they are a means of obtaining not only accurate but also objective evidence; objective because all agree as to the reading of the instrument. If there is no acceptable measuring instrument objective agreement is less likely[7] and there is no longer a clear distinction between the two languages. For example, intelligence is a quality which is not yet measured by any generally agreed and acceptable method; so assessments of intelligence are partly subjective.[8] In the biological and human sciences generally there is not the clear-cut objectivity that we get in chemistry, astronomy or physics.[9]

The human sciences seek knowledge of events that have to be described in value-loaded language; such language cannot be avoided. Unfortunately we have no way of making objective measurements of value, and therefore we cannot get a basis of agreed value-measured facts, i.e. facts with value overtones assessed by some accepted, and therefore objective standard. Even attempts to get an agreed basis for pragmatic values are only partially successful; economists relate value to price (the price is, after all, something that normally commands agreement).[10] But is the (pragmatic) value of a commodity the same as (or related to) its price? Water has a much lower price than diamonds but its value to us is far greater. And when we are considering moral values price is much less relevant; Oscar Wilde described the cynic as 'a man who knows the price of everything and the value of nothing'.[11] It is

24

because value can be distinguished from price that the epigram has impact. The biblical Proverb, 'Who can find a virtuous woman? for her price is far above rubies,'[12] which appears to relate value (pragmatic *and* moral) to price, is, in effect, putting the value beyond price.

Clearly the facts which influence and are influenced by our moral judgments cannot be firm in the sense that their value element is not fixed. This makes moral evaluation very difficult because, if we aspire to some degree of objectivity, it is necessary to at least have the possibility of inter-subjective agreement and this requires *for a start* agreement as to the relevant facts. Moral discussion of actual situations and people must start from an empirical description and this is inevitably value-loaded – it cannot be neutral. It is because moral debate is based on accounts that must beg the question (for or against) that it can easily degenerate from rational discussion to non-rational rhetoric. Disputants seek to *cause* their adversaries to change their views rather than trying to give reasons for a different moral assessment. Some philosophers have argued that there can be no *rational* and purely moral argument, that moral judgments are primarily no more than expressions of emotion and that rational discussion of moral principles is impossible. We shall consider this view, and some other views as to the nature of moral judgments, in the next chapter.

IV

EMOTIVISM AND PRESCRIPTIVISM

We shall begin by considering the views of those who do not regard moral evaluations as true judgments at all because they believe that moral judgments do not make assertions, and that therefore they are not genuine statements. Two different schools of moral philosophy are associated with this view: emotivists and prescriptivists. As we shall see, the creed of the second school has developed from that of the first.

According to emotivists, value judgments such as 'X is evil' and 'It is right to do Y' are, fundamentally, nothing more than expressions of feeling (emotion), and any individual making such 'judgments' is *primarily* evincing his or her feelings. It follows that a 'judgment' cannot be said to be true or false any more than a sigh of regret, a cry of pain, an outburst of laughter or a yawn can be said to be true or false. Just as laughter *expresses* amusement and a yawn *expresses* boredom, so 'X is evil' *expresses* moral disapproval. In his *Language, Truth and Logic* Professor Sir Alfred Ayer presents the emotivist position. He stresses that moral value judgments can be used as genuine statements if they function as descriptions: used in this way they may describe what is legal, or what most people in the nation (or particular social group) think is right or wrong. For example 'Cock fighting is wrong' is being used descriptively if it is equivalent to 'Cock fighting is illegal' or 'Cock fighting is disapproved of by most people in England today'. These statements can be shown to be true (or false) by seeing what the law *is*, or by finding out (perhaps by Gallup poll) what expressions of moral feeling the English in fact evince on this subject.

But if the statement 'Cock fighting is wrong' is being used

normatively, the speaker does not mean that it is illegal (which it is) or that most contemporary English people disapprove of it (which they probably do) but that cock fighting just is morally wrong. The speaker would wish to change the law if the law did not forbid it, and would regard public opinion as irrelevant, as far as the moral principles were concerned. The point is made clearer if we say 'hunting' instead of 'cock fighting'. Now, according to emotivists, to make the moral judgment 'Cock fighting is wrong' is to do nothing more than to *express* or *evince* moral disapproval. A person saying this no more makes a statement than if she had said 'Ouch', or 'Ooh' or 'Ah'. So Ayer concludes that words like 'right' and 'wrong', *when used normatively*,* have no real meaning; they are unanalysable and stand for pseudo-concepts. It follows that these words do not add anything to the factual content of a statement.

> Thus if I say to someone, 'You acted wrongly in stealing that money,' I am not stating anything more than if I had simply said, 'You stole that money,' in a peculiar tone of horror, or written it with the addition of some special exclamation marks. The tone, or the exclamation marks, adds nothing to the literal meaning of the sentence. It merely serves to show that the expression of it is attended by certain feelings in the speaker.
>
> If now I generalise my previous statement and say, 'Stealing money is wrong,' I produce a sentence which has no factual meaning – that is, expresses no proposition which can be either true or false. It is as if I had written 'Stealing money!!' – where the shape and thickness of the exclamation marks show, by a suitable convention, that a special sort of moral disapproval is the feeling which is being expressed. . . . I am not making any factual statement, not even a statement about my own state of mind. I am merely expressing certain moral sentiments.[1]

It is to be noted that Ayer disassociates himself, and emotivists generally, from subjectivists. Subjectivists say that moral expressions *are* statements, they are statements about the personal feelings of the individual. Ayer allows that an expression can provide such information (after all, when I say 'Ouch', others may rightly infer that I am in pain) but he stresses that the *primary* function is expression, not assertion. Moral sentiments are usually expressed in words but they do not have to be; they may be expressed by a look of disdain, contempt or admiration. All such expressions will indeed convey information about feelings to any observers just as feelings of pain, fear, surprise etc. are expressed in gestures and also can convey information. But in all these cases the *expression* of the feeling can be distinguished from any *information* that may be inferred from the behaviour. Ayer is at pains to make a firm distinction between expressing and informing because he wants to make clear that for emotivists ethical 'judgments' do not assert *anything*, not even the nature of their author's feelings.

> . . . the expression of a feeling assuredly does not always involve the assertion that one has it. And this is the important point to grasp in considering the distinction between our theory and the ordinary subjectivist theory. For whereas the subjectivist holds that ethical statements actually assert the existence of certain feelings, we hold that ethical statements are expressions and excitants of feeling which do not necessarily involve any assertion.[2]

It may seem that Ayer would contend that there could not be any rational debate on ethical matters; but this is not so for he believes that ethical debate is about the relevance of facts in the circumstances of the case debated. What he will not allow is that it is possible to discuss the moral values themselves. It is not possible just because moral concepts are pseudo-concepts and attempts to set up debates about moral values are therefore futile.

Wittgenstein agreed that moral discourse cannot be rational, in the sense that it cannot be supported by logic or by empirical evidence and so might be held to be nonsensical. But he thought that this reflected *our* limitations and in particular the restriction of our thoughts and feelings by language. We cannot get out of the cage that language makes for our concepts, and so we cannot transcend our world of facts; and our framework of human logic. However, this does not mean that moral discussion is to be dismissed as a waste of time; Wittgenstein respected those who tried to make moral evaluations even though he thought that the attempts are and must be in vain:

> Now when this is urged against me, I at once see clearly, as it were in a flash of light, not only that no description that I can think of would do to describe what I mean by absolute value, but that I would reject every significant description that

anybody could possibly suggest, *ab initio*, on the ground of its
significance. That is to say: I see now that these nonsensical
expressions [moral judgments J.T.] were not nonsensical
because I had not yet found the correct expressions, but that
their nonsensicality was their very essence. For all I wanted to
do with them was just *to go beyond* the world and that is to say
beyond significant language. My whole tendency and I believe
the tendency of all men who ever tried to write or talk Ethics
. . . was to run against the boundaries of language. This running
against the wall of our cage is perfectly, absolutely hopeless.
Ethics so far as it springs from the desire to say something about
the ultimate meaning of life, the absolute good, the absolute
valuable, can be no science. What it says does not add to our
knowledge in any sense. But it is a document of a tendency in
the human mind which I personally cannot help respecting
deeply and I would not for my life ridicule it.[3]

Wittgenstein admired the aspirations that underlie moral sentiments and moral discussion. But he concluded, reluctantly, that it
was nonsensical, admirable nonsense, but nonsense nevertheless.

Now whatever view we take of moral discussion, whether or not
we agree with Ayer and Wittgenstein, we shall agree that moral
discourse has some effect on others. Ayer himself says, 'It is worth
mentioning that ethical terms do not serve only to express feelings.
They are calculated to arouse feeling, and so to stimulate action.'[4]
But if we think that ethical terms are non-rational, standing for
pseudo-concepts, and that discussion of moral principles and moral
values cannot be rational, the arousal that moral judgments evoke
must also be non-rational. Moral judgments arouse feelings only,
and so any stimulus to action cannot be through rational argument
but must be by emotional persuasion. This is the technique of the
advertiser, the politician and the demagogue; it is often misleading
and can be dangerous.

The use of non-rational persuasion in advertisements is exempli-
fied in many TV commercials: for a shampoo where a good-looking
girl is shown floating through a hazy rural/romantic scene pervaded
by soothing musack; she meets a handsome young man, a fairy
prince, captivated by her charms. The virtues of the shampoo are
cooed but the implication is clear – buy it and you too will be
good-looking, you too will find a fairy prince. Breakfast cereal

advertisements show a cheerful, attractive, well-dressed family, with well-behaved, cutely cheeky children, sitting in a bright kitchen; buy the cereal and buy a prosperous and happy family life. Of course most advertisements contain factual information that may help to sell and it is also true that if a product is inferior to its competitors it will not do so well in the long run. The problem facing makers of shampoo, breakfast cereal and a host of other consumer goods is that others are producing almost identical commodities at much the same price; so to sell their brand they need to include a packet of free dreams. Advertising agents are aware of this; they understand the importance of discovering what the dreams of the potential buyers are.

It is the emotivist view that moral judgments are essentially non-rational that worries prescriptivists. Prescriptivism was first advocated by the Oxford philosopher Professor Richard Hare. Like Ayer, Hare does not regard value judgments as statements that can be said to be true or false but he thinks that they are more than mere *expressions* of approval or of disapproval, they are also intended as guides to behaviour and/or as guides to action. Hence they have a prescriptive character. In addition he argues that the guidance is not based on a non-rational appeal to feelings, for reasons can be given for the judgments. As Donald Hudson puts it:

> They are of the opinion that a little reflection upon moral discourse as it actually occurs will show quite clearly that it is far from being irrationalist in character. In it reasons are given for what is said; and distinctions are drawn between good reasons and bad ones, between conclusions which follow and ones which do not. A theory which appears to put morality beyond reason flies in the face of these facts.[5]

Hare wants to distinguish the emotivist view that moral attitudes are *caused* to change from the prescriptivist view that they change for *reasons*. The point is that an event (including a human action or belief) which is *caused* does not occur as a result of reasoned thought; for example if I was pushed the push might *cause* me to fall; likewise if I am non-rationally swayed by an emotive expression I shall be caused to censure an action, say abortion, as immoral. By contrast I may act or have beliefs for reasons; for example, I might decide to jump into a lake because I saw someone in distress and I might decide that abortion was wrong because I held it to be murder. In both these cases my reasons are based on valuing human life and this could be argued to be a rational and not an emotional belief.

Hare says that moral value words such as 'right' and 'ought' have what he calls a 'supervenient character' – that is they have an extra 'something' that distinguishes them from non-value words such as 'red' or 'square'. The 'extra' depends on the fact that we can always demand to know why something is right or why something ought to be done. This is a different sort of question from asking why something is red or square because we are asking for a *reason* for us to concur in the judgment. The supervenient character of moral (and aesthetic) evaluations can be shown by comparing 'This book is exactly like that one save that this has a red cover' and 'This action is exactly like that one save that this is (morally) right'.

Hare also stresses another feature of moral prescriptions, namely that they are universalisable, i.e. they must apply to everyone and must be accepted as guides to behaviour by everyone, *including those who prescribe*. Of course we are all aware that we may say 'X ought to be done', or 'X is right' and fail to act, but this does not weaken the prescriptivist position because failure to do what we know should be done engenders a feeling of guilt – we are aware of a moral lapse. If there is no feeling of guilt, then we are unaware of any moral lapse and in such cases only two explanations are possible: either the judgment is not accepted – for example a person might not accept the judgment 'It is wrong to eat animals' – or it is not understood – for example a person might not understand the reasons for the judgment 'It is wrong to offer sweets to unknown children', and therefore could make such offers without feeling guilty.

But universalisability still presents problems. Hare considers an extreme case: the Nazi who says that all Jews ought to be exterminated. He says that only a fanatic would accept such a judgment if he or she were Jewish. He contends that the test of universalisability remains valid because there are only very small numbers of fanatics who will be prepared to accept the consequences for themselves (as well as for all others) of acting on an immoral judgment. The views of these fanatics can be disregarded, he says.

Not all philosophers agree with him; Geoffrey Warnock says that just because someone might not want to accept the consequences of a judgment for himself (or herself), i.e. the judgment was *not* universalisable, it does not necessarily follow that he or she thought that the judgment was wrong. There are plenty of examples: the torture of terrorists to extract information might not be acceptable to a terrorist but he might think it was a right judgment; the eviction of tenants who fail to pay rent might not be wanted by a defaulter though she might admit the rule was right; the abortion of an unwanted foetus might not be acceptable to the foetus (if it could express itself) though it might (if it were able) concede the morality of such abortions. Warnock charges Hare with equivocating:

> It is true . . . that no rational man *wants* the frustration of what he sees as his own interests, or *likes* it when his interests are frustrated. But then what a man wants, or would like, is scarcely the point at issue here: the question is what he would morally approve or find morally objectionable; and that, of course, may not be at all the same thing.[6]

Warnock is arguing that whether a judgment is or is not universally accepted does not tell us whether it is (or is not) right because *wants* cannot be equated with what is right.

Hare himself has in effect conceded this for he points out that there are situations that are regarded as immoral even though everyone's wants are satisfied:

> Consider the questions . . . of whether it is wrong for a pretty girl to earn good money by undressing herself at a 'strip club' for the pleasure of middle-aged business-men. If this is not a moral question in an accepted sense of the word, it is hard to say what would be. The enlightened may not think it very important. Yet those who call such exhibitions immoral do not do so because of their effect on other people's interests; for, since everybody gets what he or she wants, nobody's interests are harmed. They are likely, rather, to use such words as 'degrading'. This gives us a clue to the sort of moral question with which we are dealing. It is a question not of interests but of *ideals*. Such conduct offends against an ideal of human excellence. . . . one reason why it is wrong to confine the term 'moral question' by terminological fiat to questions concerning the effect of our actions upon other people's interests, is that such a restriction would truncate moral philosophy by preventing it saying anything about ideals.[7]

Hare proposes that there should be a distinction between what it is good to do and what we ought to do: failure to do good (or *be* good) is not necessarily to be immoral, and this is related to the idealist aspect of conduct. By contrast, failure to do as we ought is *moral* failure because it is a failure in duty and concerns the interests of others. He says, 'The conclusion . . . of our discussion of ideals seems to be this. Where interests are not concerned, conflicts between ideals are not susceptible to very much in the way of argument.'[8] Thus in so far as 'good' is concerned (as in considering the morality of a striptease show), there are not necessarily any universalisable moral principles; but that in relation to *duty*, what we *ought* to do, there are such principles and morality is not a matter of individual choice. Hare says that we find what principles are acceptable by exploring their consequences and he compares moral reasoning to scientific reasoning:

> We must ask whether moral reasoning exhibits any similar features. I want to suggest that it too is a kind of exploration. . . What we are doing in moral reasoning is to look for moral judgments and moral principles which, when we have considered their logical consequences and the facts of the case, we can still accept.[9]

And a little later:

> The rules of moral reasoning are, basically, two, corresponding to the two features of moral judgments . . . prescriptivity and universalizability. When we are trying, in a concrete case, to decide what we ought to do, what we are looking for . . . is an action to which we can commit ourselves (prescriptivity) but which we are at the same time prepared to accept as exemplifying a principle of action to be prescribed for others in like circumstances (universalizability). If, when we consider some proposed action, we find that, when universalized, it yields prescriptions which we cannot accept, we reject this action as a solution to our moral problem – if we cannot universalize the prescription, it cannot become an 'ought'.[10]

So, we judge that an action is universalisable by appeal to consequences and by appeal to moral principles, themselves *justified* by consequences. But Hare does not say that actual (or putative) consequences make moral judgments true or false because he does not think that such judgments make assertions. By contrast consequentialists hold that moral judgments do make assertions and that they are therefore expressed as genuine statements. Hence they can be true (or false), and that truth (or falsity) is established by appeal to the consequences of acting on the judgment. We turn to their views in the next chapter.

V

CONSEQUENTIALISM: HAPPINESS AND JUSTICE

Consequentialists hold that moral judgments are statements that can be judged true or false by appeal to the observed, or potentially observable or putative consequences. Thus they think that moral value judgments are a form of empirical statement, i.e. statements of matters of fact.

Utilitarianism is the consequentialist doctrine that takes as its basic premise that it is *self-evident* that everyone desires happiness and that everyone wishes to avoid unhappiness. Thus actions that increase happiness (or decrease unhappiness) are good and actions that decrease happiness (or increase unhappiness) are evil. It was first promulgated by Jeremy Bentham (1748–1832) and was primarily directed at promoting a new view of legislation. His advocacy of utilitarianism was associated with the then radical view that every individual's happiness was of equal value and that the law should respect the rights and needs of the poor as much as those of the prosperous. It was John Stuart Mill (1806–73) who developed the doctrine to apply not only to legislation but also to personal morality. In relation to the latter the dominant nineteenth-century view was that we had the capacity to know what was right or wrong in virtue of moral intuition; it was clearly related to Ancient Greek and early Christian views and, as we shall see, had been given a secular base, or at least one free from overt appeal to Christianity, by Kant. Mill objected to intuitionism not because he did not believe there was any such capacity, but because he thought that intuitionists either followed a multiplicity of principles (and he thought there should be just one), or, as in the case of Kant, the one principle suggested could support outrageously immoral conduct –

35

conduct that would be rejected because we would not choose to incur the consequences. Writing of Kant, he said:

> This remarkable man, whose system of thought will long remain one of the landmarks in the history of philosophical speculation, does, in the treatise in question, lay down a universal principle as the origin and ground of moral obligation; it is this: – 'So act, that the rule on which thou actest would admit of being adopted as a law by all rational beings.' But when he begins to deduce from this precept any of the actual duties of morality, he fails, almost grotesquely, to show that there would be any contradiction, any logical (not to say physical) impossibility, in the adoption by all rational beings of the most outrageously immoral conduct. All he shows is that the *consequences* of their universal adoption would be such as no one would choose to incur.[1]

Mill pointed out that the ultimate end of actions (judged morally) must be acknowledged to be *self-evidently good*, that is good without any further appeal for support, and he thought there was only one such end, embodied in the Principle of Utility or Greatest Happiness Principle. He took happiness to be much the same as pleasure: 'By happiness is intended pleasure and the absence of pain; by unhappiness, pain and the privation of pleasure.'[2]

Utilitarianism aroused opposition for several different reasons. We should not underestimate the contemporary opposition based on the view, strong though rarely expressed publicly, that society required the happiness of the well-to-do to be of more account than the happiness of the poor. There was also opposition on religious grounds; it was argued that the utilitarian view of morality was too hedonistic and too secular in that the pleasures anticipated were the pleasures of this world rather than the next. This objection is related to the criticism based on the view that the Principle of Greatest Happiness was degrading human aspirations; we shall return to this later. Let us first consider an objection which I think Mill successfully counters, namely the view that his utilitarian morality was mere hedonism. Defending his thesis he says:

> Now, such a theory of life excites in many minds, and among them in some of the most estimable in feeling and purpose, inveterate dislike. To suppose that life has (as they express it) no

36

higher end than pleasure– no better and nobler object of desire and pursuit – they designate as utterly mean and grovelling; a doctrine worthy only of swine, to whom the followers of Epicurus were at a very early period, contemptuously likened; and modern holders of the doctrine are occasionally made the subject of equally polite comparisons by its German, French and English assailants.

When thus attacked, the Epicureans have always answered, that it is not they, but their accusers, who represent human nature in a degrading light; since the accusation supposes human beings to capable of no pleasures except those of which swine are capable. . . . But there is no known Epicurean theory of life which does not assign to the pleasures of the intellect, of the feelings and imagination, and of the moral sentiments, a much higher value as pleasures than those of mere sensation. . . . It is quite compatible with the principle of utility to recognise the fact, that some *kinds* of pleasure are more desirable and more valuable than others.[3]

For Mill happiness was best attained by cultivating the higher faculties:

Of two pleasures, if there be one to which all or almost all who have experience of both give a decided preference, irrespective of any feeling of moral obligation to prefer it, that is the most desirable pleasure. . . . we are justified in ascribing to the preferred enjoyment a superiority in quality. . . .

Now it is an unquestionable fact that those who are equally acquainted with, and equally capable of appreciating and enjoying, both, do give a most marked preference to the manner of existence which employs their higher faculties. Few human creatures would consent to be changed into any of the lower animals, for the promise of the fullest allowance of a beast's pleasures; no intelligent human being would consent to be a fool, no instructed person would be an ignoramus, no person of feeling and conscience would be selfish and base, even though they be persuaded that the fool, the dunce, or the rascal is better satisfied with his lot than they are with theirs. . . . It is better to be a human being dissatisfied than a pig satisfied; better to be Socrates dissatisfied than a fool satisfied. And if the fool or the pig are of a different opinion, it is because they only know their own side of the question. The other party to the comparison knows both sides.[4]

and:

> It may be questioned whether anyone who has remained equally susceptible to both classes of pleasures, ever knowingly and calmly preferred the lower; though many, in all ages, have broken down in an ineffectual attempt to combine both.[5]

It is less easy to answer the charge that utilitarianism is potentially degrading. At this point we need to distinguish the utilitarian justification of legislation from its criterion of the truth of judgments of personal morality. In the former case, utilitarianism does seem, at least on first assessment, to offer a fair justification of legislation: it can justify laws giving equal rights regardless of colour, religion and sex; it can justify laws to raise taxes; it can justify compulsory insurance and the need for bureaucracy to implement those laws; it can justify laws to do with road safety and laws to do with the restricting of drugs. There is disagreement about what *does* promote social happiness and what the consequences of a given law may be but as a social principle utilitarianism commands much support. If we accept the Benthamite view our difficulties are in finding out how best to achieve the goal of maximum happiness, but this is a social and psychological problem, not a moral one.

In defending his view that utilitarianism was the best basis for personal morality Mill related it to Christian principles:

> I must again repeat, what the assailants of utilitarianism seldom have the justice to acknowledge, that the happiness which forms the utilitarian standard of what is right in conduct, is not the agent's own happiness, but that of all concerned. As between his own happiness and that of others, utilitarianism requires him to be as strictly impartial as a disinterested and benevolent spectator. In the golden rule of Jesus of Nazareth, we read the complete spirit of the ethics of utility. To do as you would be done by, and to love your neighbour as yourself, constitute the ideal perfection of utilitarian morality.[6]

And he continues;

> I know not what recommendation possessed by any other morality they could possibly affirm to be wanting to it; what

more beautiful or more exalted developments of human nature any other ethical system can be supposed to foster, or what springs of action, not accessible to the utilitarian, such systems rely on for giving effect to their mandates.[7]

But objectors to utilitarian standards were not satisfied; they were concerned to show, firstly, that happiness should not be an end in itself, and secondly, that it was, in any case, unattainable. Mill replied robustly:

> Against this doctrine arises another class of objectors, who say that happiness in any form, cannot be the rational purpose of human life and action; because, in the first place, it is unattainable: and they contemptuously ask, what right hast thou to be happy? a question which Mr Carlyle clenches by the addition, What right, a short time ago, hast thou even *to be*? Next, they say, that men can do without happiness; that all noble human beings have felt this, and could not have become noble but by learning the lesson of Entsagen, of renunciation; which lesson, thoroughly learned and submitted to, they affirm to be the beginning and necessary condition of all virtue.[8]

Mill pointed out that even if happiness were unattainable this would not count against utilitarianism for utilitarianism also valued the reduction of unhappiness; but anyway the objection smacked of verbal quibble, or, at the least, gross exaggeration – for happiness was something more than pleasurable excitement. He conceded, sarcastically, that it was certainly possible to do without happiness, as nineteen-twentieths of mankind did without it involuntarily. He also granted that the occasional hero or martyr sacrificed happiness voluntarily but, he said, the whole point of their sacrifice was to increase the happiness of others.

> All honour to those who can abnegate for themselves the personal enjoyment of life, when by such renunciation they contribute worthily to increase the amount of happiness in the world; but he who does it, or professes to do it, for any other purpose is no more deserving of admiration than the ascetic mounted on his pillar. He may be an inspiring proof of what men *can* do, but assuredly not an example *of* what they *should*.[9]

However Carlyle's objection, that pleasure or happiness *should not* be our *ultimate* end, and the ultimate criterion for assessing a moral judgment, is not easily dismissed; for it seems to be an empirical fact that happiness, taken as the satisfaction of desires, is inadequate. Human well-being seems to require something to strive for, a something that may well be unattainable so that there is never smug complacency but rather the opposite, an element of discontent, a feeling that more could and should be achieved. This is not to disparage the work of those who seek to improve the lot of others by trying to create a society where there are more material goods for those in need, but to maintain that this alone is not enough. *Brave New World* is a satire of a consumer society that has no aspirations beyond the material and the sensual, and where discontent is not *allowed* to develop;

> Hot tunnels alternated with cool tunnels. Coolness was wedded to discomfort in the form of hard X-rays. By the time they were decanted the embryos had a horror of cold. They were predestined to emigrate to the tropics, to be miners and acetate silk spinners and steel workers. Later their minds would be made to endorse the judgment of their bodies. 'We condition them to thrive on heat,' . . . 'Our colleagues upstairs will teach them to love it.'
>
> 'And that,' put in the Director sententiously, 'that is the secret of happiness and virtue – liking what you've *got* to do. All conditioning aims at that: making people like their inescapable destiny.'[10]

And later:

> 'I suppose Epsilons don't really mind being Epsilons,' she said aloud.
>
> 'Of course they don't. How can they? They don't know what it's like being any thing else. We'd mind, of course. But then we've been differently conditioned. Besides we start with a different heredity.'
>
> 'I'm glad I'm not an Epsilon,' said Lenina with conviction.
>
> 'And if you were an Epsilon,' said Henry, 'your conditioning would have made you no less thankful that you weren't a Beta or an Alpha.'

....

He sighed. Then in a resolutely cheerful voice, 'Anyhow' . . . 'there's one thing we can be certain of whoever he may have been, he was happy when he was alive. Everybody's happy now.' 'Yes, everybody's happy now,' echoed Lenina. They had heard the words repeated a hundred and fifty times every night for twelve years.[11]

These passages are satirical because we do not want to be conditioned to like what we get; we *want to have the capacity to be dissatisfied*, and purely pleasurable experiences are not enough. Finnis shows this by describing a thought-experiment proposed by Robert Nozick:

Suppose you could be plugged into an 'experience machine' which, by stimulating your brain while you lay floating in a tank, would afford you all the experiences you choose, with all the variety (if any) you could want: but you must plug in for a lifetime or not at all. On reflection, is it not clear, first, that you would not choose a lifetime of 'thrills' or 'pleasurable tingles' or other experiences of that type? But, secondly, is it not clear that one would not choose the *experiences* of discovering an important theorem, or of winning an exciting game, or of sharing a satisfying friendship, or of reading or writing a great novel, or even of seeing God . . . or any combination of such experiences? The fact is, is it not, that if one were sensible one would not choose to plug into the experience machine *at all*. For, as Nozick rightly concludes, one wants to *do* certain things (not just have the experience of doing them); one wants to *be* a certain sort of person, through one's own authentic free self-determination and self-realisation; one wants to *live* (in the active sense) oneself, making a real world through that real pursuit of values that inevitably involves making one's personality in and through one's free commitment to those values.[12]

Mill himself would have been horrified at *Brave New World*, for though he had said that happiness was equivalent to pleasure his writings show clearly that he believed that an essential part of the happiness of rational human beings consisted in making their own decisions, i.e. in acting autonomously. In *On Liberty* he said:

Nobody denies that people should be so taught and trained in

41

youth as to know and benefit by the ascertained results of human experience. But it is the privilege and proper condition of a human being, arrived at the maturity of his faculties, to use and interpret experience in his own way.[13]

Moreover that power of rational choice must be exercised:

The human faculties of perception, judgement, discriminative feeling, mental activity, and even moral preference, are exercised only in making a choice. He who does anything because it is the custom makes no choice. He gains no practice either in discerning or in desiring what is best. The mental and moral life, like the muscular powers, are improved only by being used.[14]

Mill would have utterly repudiated the Nozick experience machine since he understood happiness (pleasure) as an activity. John Gray says:

The abstractness and complexity of Mill's conception of happiness represents the attempt in a spirit of psychological realism to come to grips with the diversity and variety of human purposes and to identify happiness with the successful pursuit of self-chosen goals rather than with the having of any sort of sensation.[15]

In Gray's view Mill's utilitarianism presupposes a complex notion of happiness (pleasure) and his criticism of Mill's doctrine is that it fails to give practical guidance as to how competing elements of pleasure are to be weighed.[16]

Another problem for Mill and for utilitarians generally is the assessment of the role of paternalism in moral behaviour. We can assume that there is such a thing as a genuine paternalism, i.e. actions performed with the sincere intention of benefiting another. It follows that a person who acts altruistically does not necessarily act so as to give another what that other desires; an altruistic action is one that she sees as being in the *best interests* of another (or of others) – the interests of others being given more weight than the interests of the agent. Naturally the agent may take a wrong decision and it may turn out that the altruistic action was *not* in the best interests of others after all, but here we are concerned with intentions. An altruist acts so as to further what she genuinely thinks are the best interests of someone else. We have to concede that such altruism overrides the autonomy of the beneficiary and therefore cannot be commended without qualification, nevertheless we admire those who are sincerely concerned to put the interests of others before their own interests.

To say that all human beings need to strive, to aspire, is not to say that material deprivation is therefore good or in the best interest of people in general. It is simply to stress that an adequate, even luxurious supply of goods and services cannot, by itself, make a full life. Nor is success, including complete satisfaction (see quote 15 above) of intellectual and aesthetic needs (Mill's 'higher pleasures') all we seem to require. The nature of intellectual and aesthetic pleasure demands active participation and precludes the possibility of reaching a point where no further effort is required; we seem to need a target or goal always a little ahead. Professor Anthony O'Hear goes further: he suggests that human beings need to *suffer*, not just to strive:

> I am claiming that suffering and weakness are central and
> essential aspects of human life, and that most of what we find
> admirable in human life involves in some part an acceptance of
> suffering and the conquest of evil. (I am not, of course, saying
> that we should not strive to eliminate suffering as far as we can;
> but rather that we should, at the same time, strive to come to
> terms with its inevitability) . . . whatever else it would be, a
> totally rational and pleasant life, without suffering and
> wickedness, would not be a human life.[17]

And later he suggests that human achievements could not have been what they are without suffering:

> Moreover, as I have already suggested, the suffering we find in
> man and in nature is so much part of human experience and so
> integral a part of the fabric of our lives that even if there is a
> sense in which we can call much of it gratuitous (i.e. *we* can see
> no point to it), a world without it would be a world in which life
> would be unimaginably different. . . . Some will no doubt
> object that this world could have provided the basis for all the
> achievements there have been in it with considerably less
> gratuitous suffering than there actually is in it. Unfortunately, I
> am unable to discover the basis on which such judgements are
> made.[18]

It would seem that the utilitarian moral criterion is psychologically self-defeating, and the utilitarian undermines her own doctrine if she insists that unhappiness is part of happiness. The fact is that people not only seem to *need* some difficulties, and perhaps sorrow, they do not have happiness as their sole ultimate aim; as Nowell-Smith says, 'The theory that men can only aim at their own happiness is plausible only when "happiness" is covertly used as a general word covering "whatever men aim at".'[19]

Today there is also criticism of utilitarianism not only as a guide to personal morality but also as a social and political doctrine. Professor Sir Stuart Hampshire argues that up to the First World War, and perhaps even until 1939, utilitarianism 'was still a bold, innovative, even a subversive doctrine, with a record of successful social criticism behind it'.[20] Hampshire does not want to rate renunciation higher than pleasure but he does believe that it is morally objectionable to take the *feeling* of pleasure as the ultimate criterion of what is good; he argues that if only the attainment of this feeling is morally significant, then morality as a system of rights and duties becomes 'a kind of psychical engineering, which shows the way to induce desired or valued states of mind'.[21] In addition, Hampshire says, the consequence of adopting the utilitarian creed would be that political action planned for the long-term benefit of mankind would become a matter of cold-blooded cost/benefit calculation:

> Persecutions, massacres and wars have been coolly justified by calculations of the long-range benefit to mankind; and political pragmatists, in the advanced countries, using cost-benefit analyses prepared for them by gifted professors, continue to burn and destroy. The utilitarian habit of mind has brought with it a new abstract cruelty to politics, a dull destructive political righteousness: a mechanical, quantitative thinking, leaden academic minds setting out their moral calculations in leaden abstract prose, and more civilised and more superstitious people destroyed because of enlightened calculations that have proved wrong.[22]

He says that losses and gains of happiness (or of pleasure) are not commensurable, so that utilitarianism cannot give practical guidance; he also thinks that utilitarianism oversimplifies ethics since moral issues cannot be represented on a single scale. It may be that we have to accept that it is impossible to act morally in certain situations without flouting important moral principles. The same point is also made by Sir Isaiah Berlin in his essay 'Equality':

> Condorcet did not allow for the possibility of a collision between
> various human ends. It was left to others to emphasize the fact
> that in life as normally lived the ideals of one society and culture
> clash with those of another, and at times conflict within the same
> society and, often enough, within the moral experience of a
> single individual; that such conflicts cannot always, even in
> principle, be wholly resolved.[23]

Apart from it offering a doubtful criterion, from being an uncertain
practical guide and from oversimplifying moral issues, Hampshire
says that a major defect is that utilitarianism does not allow that
there are certain kinds of actions and behaviour that are absolutely
wrong and that could not be justified however much happiness they
could bring. It is true that utilitarianism can be used to show that it is
morally right to keep promises, to be loyal to friends, to avoid
certain kinds of killing and many other kinds of behaviour which
does not seem related to enhancing happiness; but as utilitarian
support depends always on an ultimate appeal to enhancement of
happiness (or diminishing unhappiness), utilitarians can *never* say
that some behaviour is *wrong*, in an absolute sense. Hampshire
thinks that the effect of utilitarianism is to lower the barriers of
absolute moral prohibition:

> When the generally respected barriers of impermissible conduct
> are once crossed, and when no different unconditional barriers
> within the same areas of conduct, are put in their place, then the
> special, apparently superstitious, value attached to the
> preservation of human life will be questioned . . . it is not clear
> that the taking of lives can be marked and evaluated on a
> common scale on which increases of pleasure and diminutions of
> suffering are also measured. This is the suggested discontinuity
> which a utilitarian must deny.[24]

The taking of human life does not have any exceptional moral
implications for utilitarians – if there is no loss of happiness there is
no horror in loss of life and if general happiness is increased (or
unhappiness diminished) then loss of life is to be applauded:

> The error of the optimistic utilitarian is that he carries the
> deritualisation of transactions between men to a point at which

men not only can, but ought to use and exploit each other as
they use and exploit any other natural objects, as far as this is
compatible with general happiness.[25]

As we shall see, for utilitarians human beings cease to be 'ends in
themselves' in the Kantian sense.

Professor Bernard Williams also regards utilitarianism as, at the
last, morally debasing, and he says that this is because utilitarianism
has no place for what he calls 'moral cost':

> Utilitarianism, which hopes (in some of its indirect forms) to
> appeal to habits of reluctance, cannot in fact make any sense of
> them at this level, because it lacks a sense of *moral* cost, as
> opposed to costs of some other kind (such as utility) which have
> to be considered in arriving at a moral decision.[26]

Later he argues that Utilitarians use the Principle of Utility to
justify their moral attitudes; those attitudes do not arise from the
Principle: 'Modern Utilitarians are conformist; they are trying to
reconcile utilitarianism to *existing* moral beliefs, not using them to
reject these and replace them by others.'[27] Williams believes that
utilitarianism does not give good grounds for moral judgments and,
like Hampshire, he believes that today it can undermine morality.

These are grave charges, but there is more to be said for utilitarianism than that it had a beneficial influence on laws and attutudes in
the nineteenth and early twentieth century. The case for Mill's
thesis is taken up by Lord Quinton. He grants that a simple equation
of happiness with pleasure is unsatisfactory, but, though he thinks
that Mill does not completely rebut this objection, he thinks that
Mill did make an attempt to give some content to the concept of
happiness and that we can take pleasure to be at least an essential
ingredient of happiness:

> . . . the Benthamite definition of happiness as a sum of
> pleasures is far too neat and simple to be adequate. Mill does
> not explicitly dissent . . . but he comes near to undermining it
> when he says that for happiness men need both tranquillity, and
> excitement, in which intense pleasure is likely but with the
> added risk of much pain.

However, utilitarianism can easily survive the rejection of
Bentham's over-simplified additive reduction of happiness to
pleasure. The inadequacy of this reduction does not mean that

happiness has to be conceived as some mysterious and unanalysable state, logically unrelated to pleasure. A man is happy to the extent that his more persistent and deep-seated desires are either satisfied or are known by him to be readily satisfiable. No aggregation of intense bodily delights can compensate for the frustration of long-term and serious desires for more than a short time. Nevertheless pleasure, in the inclusive sense of the word, remains the essential ingredient of happiness.[28]

Taking the world as it is, and people as they are, we know that two people may experience the same amount of pleasure and yet one may be much happier than the other. But in so far as we are concerned with our behaviour towards others, we can, as utilitarians, advocate actions that will tend to produce pleasure (and, therefore, happiness) or diminish pain. The connection is indirect since when we have a desire it is for something specific: a glass of champagne, to win a race or to have peace and quiet. Quinton says:

> A man who says 'Now I want some pleasure' but rejects every specific pleasant thing that is offered him – the coffee, the steak and kidney pudding, the swimming pool – not because he does not think that those particular things will please him, but because, he says, he wants pleasure in itself uncontaminated by containment in any such concrete vehicle, is talking nonsense. Pleasure, one might say, is not a stuff but a relation. One can, of course, enjoy oneself and get pleasure without being able to say precisely what it is that is pleasing about one's situation. This will commonly happen when one is doing something so familiar as to seem intrinsically uninteresting, like combing one's hair or dressing, or something that is ordinarily taken to be more or less unpleasant, like washing up or shovelling manure. But even here one is not experiencing pleasure pure and simple, one is enjoying whatever the ordinarily uninteresting or disagreeable activity one is engaged upon is.[29]

Thus happiness too must have some content; Quinton thinks that when Mill refers to the desire for pleasure he has in mind that nothing can be an object of desire unless it will be thought to be pleasant to have it (and I think we must include an anticipated *loss* of pain). Quinton says, 'Expected pleasure is a logical shadow cast by desire.'[30] In his view Mill is open to real criticism in assuming that what is desired must be *morally* desirable. We can agree that the happiness of others *ought to be* desired and Mill argues that people *do* desire this. But this is certainly not self-evident and Mill's argument is fallacious:

> No reason can be given why the general happiness is desirable, except that each person, so far as he believes it to be attainable, desires his own happiness. This, however, being a fact we have not only all the proof which the case admits of, but all which it is possible to require, that happiness is good: that each person's happiness is a good to that person, and the general happiness, therefore, a good to the aggregate of all persons.[31]

As Quinton points out, just because each person's happiness is desired by each individual it does not follow that each individual desires the happiness of everyone. Quinton compares it with dreams fascinating the dreamer: it may be that each of us is fascinated by her own dreams but it does not follow that we are all fascinated by everyone's dreams. As Quinton says, it may be a matter of prudence to want everyone to be happy but this is not a moral reason. He suggests that there is a mildly emotional feeling of benevolence which we feel for others unknown to us: we respond to appeals from victims of famine and earthquake, we sympathise with those in accidents, we feel anger at accounts of cruelty, but clearly this is not enough to establish the full-blooded benevolence required by utilitarianism.

However, Quinton does not think that Mill's 'proof' of the Principle of Utility is the 'tissue of errors' that some of its critics assert it to be. He points out that it does make a distinction between the moral and the prudential aspects of behaviour, for, to be morally good, there must be an interest in the happiness of others, as well as of oneself. In addition Quinton regards as support for the doctrine the fact that it does justify intuitive notions of what is right and wrong, though also accounting for different codes of moral behaviour in different places and at different times. He concludes:

> The hard core of morality, then, as it is ordinarily conceived, is utilitarian in character, at least negatively. Furthermore, the theory that the principle of utility is fundamentally moral affords, in conjunction with the manifest differences of belief

that there are about the causes of happiness and suffering and of circumstances in which actions and their hedonistic consequences are differently related, a coherent explanation of many of the differences of moral opinion as between differently informed or circumscribed societies. It is also a considerably more plausible reaction to the fact of large-scale moral disagreement than the subjectivist conclusion that ultimate moral convictions are simply a matter of brute unarguable preference.[32]

Quinton thinks that moral disagreement is largely disagreement about the best way to maximise happiness (or diminish unhappiness); though he knows that there is the flaw of assuming that we all *want* to maximise everyone's happiness. He does not deal with the deeper objection raised by Hampshire and Williams that the goal of maximum happiness is made more important than each individual's autonomy. But he does consider a different kind of objection, the objection of those who consider that the ultimate concern of mortality must be justice, rather than happiness. He says, 'There are principles of justice, it may be held, which are at once more certain or self-evident than the principle of utility and yet which are not compatible with it.'[33]

Now 'justice' is a complex word and involves two different notions: that of equal shares (egalitarianism) and that of treatment according to what we do for the community (meritocracy). On utilitarian grounds egalitarianism may sometimes be compatible with maximum happiness: Quinton takes the example of sharing one hundred oranges among one hundred people. Happiness will be maximised by giving each person one orange; for, if fifty people had two oranges (and the others none), the second orange would not bring so much satisfaction as the first and so there would be less happiness than if one hundred people had one orange each. The reduction in total happiness would be even greater if ten people had ten oranges each and the other ninety had none: thus egalitarianism might seem supremely compatible with utilitarianism. However there are problems with distributing even oranges: some people like oranges a great deal, others may dislike them. Let us set aside this difficulty and assume that justice and equality will be able to allow for differences in taste. But there are other factors: for example some people may have worked hard looking after the orange trees, whilst others have been sunbathing; is it not just that those who work should be entitled to more? It would not be egalitarian but it would be reward by merit. Would it or would it not make everyone happier in the long run to reward merit? Probably not, and this is where the utilitarian and the egalitarian part company and the problem of reward for merit arises:

> The practice of rewarding people in proportion to the services they actually render in augmenting utility is often described as one of treating them in accordance with their deserts. But what people deserve in the light of the results they achieve is not generally the same as what they deserve in the light of their efforts. A popular singer may intensely gratify a vast number of people at the cost of no disutility to himself at all, if, as may well be the case, he would prefer to be singing to a crowd of enraptured devotees than to be doing anything else. An unpopular epic poet, on the other hand, may toil in the most painful and arduous fashion to produce a huge, unreadable work which pleases neither him nor anyone else.[34]

A utilitarian might counter by saying that the unhappiness caused by envy would need to be counted against the extra happiness generated by higher output, but what she cannot do is to assert that equality is the *basis* of happiness for this would be to concede that it, rather than happiness, is fundamental. The egalitarian morality (justice as fair shares) *is* just that – it is expected that happiness will indeed be entailed by justice but for her, happiness is subsidiary.

A more sophisticated 'justice as fairness' morality has been offered by John Rawls. He suggests that we assume that each person is fundamentally egocentric and wishes to further her own interests but also that each person appreciates that people must live together and that others will have similar desires. In general no one wants to live in a society where all are scrambling for their own ends without restriction and therefore each person is prepared to sacrifice some immediate interests in order to secure stability. What then will be the kind of society that will bring about the most satisfaction for its members? Rawls suggests that we imagine a veil of ignorance such that no one knows what her place will be or even what kind of person she will be; we are to be ignorant of our race, sex, interests and abilities. He calls this 'the original position' and acknowledges that it is a hypothetical state. But, given this state, what then would be our preferred conception of justice? Would we tolerate any inequalities? What restrictions would we permit? Even though the original position cannot be achieved that does not detract from its power to guide us to a conception of a just society. We do not have any information about our own personal position or that of others and so we shall not be influenced by what suits our own interests. This makes it more likely that we shall agree as to what is a truly just society:

> . . . once knowledge is excluded the requirement of unanimity is not out of place and the fact that it can be satisfied is of great importance. It enables us to say of the preferred conception of justice that it represents a genuine reconciliation of interests.[35]

In arriving at the preferred conception of justice Rawls assumes that the person in the original position is rational, that she tries as best she can to advance her interests and that each would prefer more of the primary social goods rather than less. One special assumption is that a rational person will not be envious, that is, will not elect to have less in order to prevent another from having more. It is also assumed that the rational person will have a sense of justice and that this is public knowledge, so that any agreement is made sincerely and is intended to be kept. Rawls maintains that the combination of mutual disinterest and the veil of ignorance achieves the same purpose as benevolence when we come to consider what conditions would be agreed to by all. Anyone would *start* from the position that equal distribution of goods was just but also any rational person would agree to *in*equalities provided that the worse off were still better off than they would be with complete equality. But although unequal distribution of goods would be permitted in such conditions all would wish to keep equality of liberty: that everyone should have the same degree of freedom to express and act on his or her beliefs. Thus we have *two principles*: first (and most important) that basic liberties can be effectively exercised and any restriction is applied equally to all, and secondly that other goods will be distributed equally *unless* an unequal distribution makes the least fortunate better off than they would otherwise be.

Rawls links our sense of justice directly to morality and holds that anyone lacking a sense of justice, i.e. lacking moral sense, cannot be truly human:

> . . . a person who lacks a sense of justice, and who would never act as justice requires except as self-interest and expediency prompt, not only is without ties of friendship, affection and mutual trust, but is incapable of experiencing resentment and indignation. He lacks certain natural attitudes and moral feelings of a particularly elementary kind. Put another way, one who lacks a sense of justice lacks certain fundamental attitudes and capacities included under the notion of humanity.[36]

He thinks that it is our sense of justice that regulates moral education and our expressions of moral approval and disapproval. Value judgments can be shown to be true or false by appeal to the *justice* of their consequence.

There is no doubt that many moral judgments are assessed by appeal to the consequences of the behaviour they commend, but there are grave difficulties for *all* consequentialist views. One difficulty is that we cannot always predict the consequences and on many occasions cannot make more than a rough guess; a second difficulty is that any one action, or even code of behaviour, is not the sole causal factor – what happens might have happened without it, and/or what happens may be helped (or hindered) by other actions and events. There are many implications related to the first difficulty: should we judge agents by the consequences of their actions or by their *intended* consequences? And if by intentions, do we take account of folly or stupidity or carelessness? How do we assess intentions? One may be in doubt as to one's own intentions, and certainly others' may be in doubt. There are also good and bad situations that are created by chance or inadvertently. These contribute to moral luck, good and bad. In his essay 'Moral Luck', Thomas Nagel says:

> The same degree of culpability or estimability in intention, motive, or concern is compatible with a wide range of judgments, positive or negative, depending on what happened beyond the point of decision. The *mens rea* which could have existed in the absence of any consequences does not exhaust the grounds of moral judgment. Actual results influence culpability or esteem in a large class of unquestionably ethical cases ranging from negligence through political choice.
>
> That these are genuine moral judgments rather than expressions of temporary attitude is evident from the fact that

one can say *in advance* how the moral verdict will depend on the results. If one negligently leaves the bath running with the baby in it one will realize, as one bounds up the stairs towards the bathroom, that if the baby has drowned one has done something awful, whereas if it has not one has merely been careless.[37]

And later

How is it possible to be more or less culpable depending on whether a child gets into the path of one's car, or a bird into the path of one's bullet? Perhaps it is true that what is done depends on the agent's state of mind or intention. The problem then is, why is it not irrational to base moral assessments on what people do, in this broad sense? It amounts to holding them responsible for the contributions of fate as well as for their own – provided they have made some contribution to begin with. If we look at cases of negligence or attempt, the pattern seems to be that overall culpability corresponds to the product of intentional fault and the seriousness of the outcome.[38]

Nagel says that we are inclined to stay with a rational view of moral judgments, a view that gives the agent at least some responsibility and entails 'paring away' external factors so as to leave a moral core. There is a tendency to isolate the intentions of the agent from the circumstances *and* from the actual action.[39] But does this entail isolating the agent's character or disposition from her will? As we shall see, intuitionists believe that it is always possible (providing there is no physical constraint or gross mental derangement) for a person to choose how to act. They grant that some people find it easier to behave well than do others, but if these others are to be judged as human beings we must assume that they can choose to act morally.

The second defect of consequentialism as a doctrine for assessing moral judgments is that it is often very difficult to know what the consequence of an action *was*, for the observed results may arise from it *and* from other occurrences. This obviously applies to political decisions: for example did the assassination at Sarajevo cause the First World War by being necessary to tip the balance or would it have started anyway? Did the miners' strike bring down the Heath government or was it near to collapse? Similar difficulties arise in assessing the morality of everyday actions: if I am still recovering from flu and decide to go to a party am I the cause of other guests getting flu next week?

It is clear that we do judge agents by their intentions and actions by the consequences, but it is not clear that moral value judgments themselves are true or false *only* insofar as they can be shown to involve desirable (by some standard such as happiness or justice) and undesirable consequences. Nor is it clear that agents should be judged solely by the consequences they intend. Intuitionism offers a different criterion.

VI

INTUITIONISM

Intuitionists believe that human beings have an innate moral capacity analogous to, though not the same as, their intellectual capacity, which enables them to make moral value judgments and to assess them as being true or false. Just as we can understand that '2 + 2 = 4' so we can understand that 'Love thy neighbour as thyself' is a true moral judgment. Intuitionists hold that the basic moral truths are self-evident, like simple logical and mathematical truths, and that other moral truths can be demonstrated by argument from the basic premises.

Intuitionism is the oldest ethical tradition; we saw in chapter I that Aristotle thought that men had an intuitive notion of the Good and that Christian theologians such as Aquinas had the same belief. The Christian religion, and most other religions, assert that God (or the Gods) love the Good and so commands mankind to be good. But, in general, religious thinkers have followed the Greek secular tradition in maintaining that the Good is not good *because* it is divinely approved, rather it is divinely approved because it is *worthy* to be approved. The devout claim that God can help mankind to a clear view of the Good, and can help them to use their moral capacity so that they know how to live rightly.

There is no doubt that whether or no we are believers, we in Western Europe are strongly influenced by Christian tradition. Most of us would approve the morality of the New Testament, though it is worth remembering that 'Thou shalt love thy neighbour as thyself'[1] is in both the Old and the New Testaments. Other religions provide a basis for moral standards in other societies. Thus, writing in 1965, Lord Devlin says, 'Morals and religion are inextricably joined – the moral standards generally accepted in Western civilisation being those belonging to Christianity. Outside Christendom other standards derive from other religions.'[2]

The intuitionist view of moral judgments came to be questioned in the eighteenth century. At that time serious doubts as to the truth of the Christian doctrine and as to the divine origin of the Bible were arising. The dogma that predicted eternal damnation of the wicked, the virgin birth, the resurrection, the redemption and the divinity of Christ were called into question. The Scottish philosopher David Hume (1711–1776) refused to rely on Christianity and questioned the independent validity of moral judgments. Nor did he think that they were validated by an innate moral intuition or by moral reason; for Hume reason was the slave of the passions in that we made use of our rational powers to show us how to get what we desired. He said that if moral judgments were to have any objective force, as opposed to being mere subjective statements of personal opinion, they must describe what the community thought was commendable or disgraceful. This is in accord with Ayer's exposition of emotivism (see chapter IV). It will be remembered that Ayer said that if by 'This is good' we mean 'This is legal' or 'This is generally commended in our society', a genuine statement had been made, a statement that could be shown to be true or false; but otherwise such phrases were mere expressions of feeling. Though they might also happen to convey information they were, in essence, just gestures – pseudo-statements.

Intuitionists do not accept this; the Good is not good because it is legal or because it is socially approved (or even divinely approved (see page 55). Nor does a moral judgment merely state a subjective personal opinion, and neither is it merely the evincing of moral feelings. As we saw earlier, intuitionists believe that human beings know the good in virtue of their capacity for moral reason and that they have an innate ability to make moral evaluations. In the latter part of the eighteenth century Immanuel Kant (1724–1804) elaborated a secular intuitionism; he had fully appreciated Hume's criticism and yet he wanted to show that morality was more than socially approved conduct. He sought to establish a firm basis for moral judgments that was independent of social conventions and, even though he himself was a sincere Christian, was independent of religion. He stressed the intuitionist view that all human beings possessed an innate moral sense that must lead them to acknowledge the force of the moral law. This law was in the form of a command, a *categorical imperative*, that had to be obeyed without qualification. It could be expressed as:

> 'I ought never to act except in such a way that I can also will that my maxim should become a universal law'[3]

and as:

> 'Act in such a way that you always treat humanity, whether in your own person or in the person of any other, never simply as a means, but always at the same time as an end.'[4]

The first formulation is obviously compatible with the universalisability criterion demanded by prescriptivists and indeed our consideration of prescriptivism in chapter IV shows that *both* formulations are different ways of stating the same principle, for a moral judgment that is universalisable must, according to Hare, be applicable to those who make the judgment as well as all others. We saw in chapter V that Mill objected to Kant's moral principle (as expressed in the first formulation) and he would have considered that in the second formulation it embodied a covert appeal to consequences.

Certainly Kant did not want to have the truth of his moral law dependent on the consequences of its application and nor did he view that law as being a command that was justified by consequences. It was *understood* to be right by all rational persons. Kant said that there were two aspects to the human will: the heteronomous aspect was that part of the will governed by desires for sensual gratification and the goodies of this world – it was not guided by reason but used reason to achieve its ends and so, in relation to this facet of human nature, Hume had been right to say that reason was the slave of the passions. But there was also the autonomous aspect of the will, the will of the moral and rational part of human nature – this will did not command reason, it was guided by reason; in effect reason issued the commands and so moved the autonomous will to freely choose to follow the moral law. Actions were right if they conformed to the moral law; they were not to be judged by consequences:

> . . . when moral value is in question, we are concerned, not with the actions which we see, but with their inner principles, which we cannot see.

Furthermore, to those who deride all morality as the mere phantom of a human imagination which gets above itself out of vanity we can do no service more pleasing than to admit that the concepts of duty must be drawn solely from experience . . . for by so doing we prepare them for an assured triumph. . . . One need not be exactly a foe to virtue, but merely a dispassionate observer declining to take the liveliest wish for goodness straight away as its realisation, in order . . . to become doubtful whether any genuine virtue is actually to be encountered in the world. And then nothing can protect us against a complete falling away from our Ideas of duty . . . except the clear conviction that even if there never have been actions springing from such pure sources, the question at issue here is not whether this or that has happened; that on the contrary, reason by itself and independently of all appearances commands what ought to happen.[5]

If we had no moral sense and no capacity for reason we would be determined by our material desires; we would not be immoral but amoral, just like the animals; on the other hand if we were purely rational (members only of what Kant called the *intelligible world*) we would be purely moral beings and would freely choose the good. It was the conflict between the two aspects of the will – the heteronomous will of the *sensible* (of the senses) world, and the autonomous will of the intelligible world – that brought about the notion of moral obligation, the notion of 'I ought':

. . . if I were solely a member of the intelligible world all my actions would be in perfect conformity with the principle of the autonomy of a pure will; if I were solely a part of the sensible world, they would have to be taken as in complete conformity with the law of nature governing desires and inclinations. . . .

If I were solely a member of the intelligible world all my actions *would* invariably accord with the autonomy of the will; but because I intuit myself at the same time as a member of the sensible world, they *ought* so to accord. . . .

The moral 'I ought' is thus an 'I will' for man as a member of the intelligible world; and it is conceived by him as an 'I ought' only insofar as he considers himself at the same time to be a member of the sensible world.[6]

Kant's view is in accord with our straightforward intuitions about morality. In its first formulation it is an appeal to the principle of universalisability and this is what any rational person would require of a moral law. In its second formulation the categorical imperative clearly supports the moral prohibitions of common sense; it supports the condemnation of murder, rape, theft, dishonesty, fraud and tyranny. It also supports the moral feelings we have to respect the rights and interests of others and our notions of justice. Kant's imperative also stresses what we all acknowledge, that the nature of morality is quite different from that of self-interest and sensual gratification. Morality is not just one factor to be balanced against others, it overrides other considerations – it is indeed categorical.

But we may feel that by stressing the absolute independence of morality from consequences Kant has gone too far. For, by divorcing the justification of the moral law from what will happen if it is acted on, he removes an essential aspect of morality, the aspect concerned with how we, *in fact*, treat each other. A view of ethics that places morality apart from all consequences is suspect because though we do not want moral principles that are trimmed to every eventuality we do not want to have principles that are formed without *any* reference to what happens. We want general moral laws but they need to be supported by principles that are not *entirely* independent of experience. Likewise, though Kant's account of the autonomous will is attractive, we are left with a will that is unmotivated by any desire and, if the autonomous will has *no* desires, why should it will any course of action? A will that freely chooses to obey the moral law must choose for some reason if it is a rational will. The reason given by Kant, or implied by Kant, is the desire for inner worth:

There is no one, not even the most hardened scoundrel –
provided only he is accustomed to use reason in other ways –
who, when presented with examples of honesty in purpose, of
faithfulness to good maxims, of sympathy, and of kindness
towards all . . . does not wish that he too might be a man of like
spirit. . . . By such a wish he shows that having a will free from
sensuous impulses he transfers himself in thought into an order
of things quite different from that of his desires in the field of
sensibility; . . . all he can expect is a greater inner worth of his
own person.[7]

This is indeed a fine motive, and, as we saw in chapter I it is a *moral* motive, but it is a motive and can be something desired. It *is* good to desire to be virtuous, but why? Nineteenth-century utilitarianism, appealing to desire for happiness, was in part a response to Kant's appeal to the autonomous will and its free choice to follow the moral law. But we have seen that utilitarianism has grave defects; there was a return to intuitionism in the twentieth century.

Twentieth-century intuitionism is grounded on the views of the Cambridge philosopher George Moore, as presented in his *Principia Ethica* (published in 1903), though Moore himself denied that he was an intuitionist, at least in the ordinary sense. In his preface he asserted that no relevant evidence could be produced to support answers to purely ethical questions such as 'Ought something to exist for its own sake?', 'Does it have intrinsic value?', 'Is it good in itself?'. In other words, answers to these questions could not be established as true or false by appeals to logic (reason) or by appeals to observation (experience). For this reason Moore did concede that he sometimes called the answers given 'intuitions', but he did not allow that it followed that he was an intuitionist. He said that he was unlike other intuitionists in that he implied nothing as to the origins of our ethical intuitions and he was also unlike them in that he did not think that ethical intuitions were infallible: 'I hold, on the contrary, that in every way in which it is possible to cognise a true proposition, it is also possible to recognise a false one.'[8] Neverthe-less, because Moore insisted that good could only be apprehended as an intuition, he is taken as an intuitionist despite his protesta-tions. He proposed that the rightness of actions depended on whether or not they led to some good. For him the word 'right' stood for 'what is good as a means, whether or not it be also good as an end'.[9] Judgments as to the rightness of *actions* had to depend on two kinds of statement: ethical statements of what were morally good ends (believed to be good by intuition) and descriptions of actual or presumed consequences of actions – what Moore called 'causal truths', which were dependent on evidence provided by observation of human behaviour. For the latter factual knowledge of the same kind as that used for scientific judgments was needed, though Moore appreciated that true *generalised* judgments about the effects of actions were far more difficult to make than true generalised scientific judgments (scientific laws) because the re-levant circumstances were so complex. It was exceedingly difficult to arrive at ethical laws.

Moore distinguished the quality denoted by the adjective 'good' from the entity (substantive) denoted by 'that which is good'. For him the adjective 'good' stood for a simple moral quality which could not be defined; it was in that way like the simple perceptible quality denoted by 'yellow'. But 'the good' denoted the entity *to which* the quality 'good' could be applied. 'The good' could be defined; indeed, said Moore, the main reason for writing on ethics was to help discover that definition, i.e. the nature of the good.

> . . . for I deny good to be definable. I say that it is not composed of any parts, which we can substitute for it in our minds when we are thinking of it. . . .
>
> But I am afraid I will have still not removed the chief difficulty which may prevent acceptance of the proposition that good is indefinable. I do not mean to say that *the* good, that which is good, is thus indefinable; if I did think so, I should not be writing Ethics, for my main object is to help towards discovering that definition. It is just because I think there will be less risk of error in our search for a definition of 'the good', that I am now insisting that *good* is indefinable.[10]

Moore believed that failure to appreciate the difference between *good* and *the good* had hindered progress in ethical study. For example, said Moore, it may be that pleasure is good and some people (Moore had Bentham and Mill in mind) have said 'only pleasure is good'; they think that they have defined *good* by equating it with pleasure. But *even if* the statement '*Only* pleasure is good' were true, goodness has not been defined, only *the good*, or that which is good. He said that those who confused *good* with *the good*, which they did when they equated *good* with another quality (that they thought all good things possessed), were committing what he called 'the naturalistic fallacy'. He gave the mistake this name because he wanted to stress that the fallacy consisted in equating the non-natural quality *good* (non-natural because it was not an object of sense perception but was apprehended in the mind) with some natural (perceptible) quality such as pleasure. He wanted moral philosophers to acknowledge that they had to have an intuitive understanding of moral goodness before they could discuss what *other* qualities good things might have.

Moore was not engaged in verbal quibbling; he had compared

'good' with 'yellow' in that yellowness was also a simple and indefinable quality (albeit a natural, perceptible, quality). Just as we can make statements about *the good* (things which are good) and also about the quality *good*, so we can make statements about yellow things and the quality yellow. We may truly say 'All yellow objects reflect light of a certain wavelength (just as we might say all good things give happiness), but this is not to say that the word 'yellow' *means* 'reflecting light of a certain wavelength' (or that the word 'good' *means* 'giving happiness'). Thus when we say 'States of happiness are good', 'Merciful acts are good', 'Just people are good', and so on, we are making statements equivalent to 'Surfaces emitting light of a certain wavelength are yellow'. The significance of the statements depends on *prior and independent* recognition of goodness (and of yellowness).

This was Moore's view and, on first consideration, it seems very acceptable: moral goodness being a simple quality intuitively apprehended and one that we must recognise before we can say that any person, action or situation is characterised by it. But is this so? Is it intuitively apprehended and is it a simple quality? We shall leave the question of intuitive apprehension till later; it suffices here to say that Moore's suggestions as to *what* had the quality of goodness (that he claimed to apprehend intuitively) – happiness, beauty, pleasure and intelligence – arose from the background of the Greek and Christian values of a cultivated Englishman. Because his readers had very similar backgrounds, and perhaps still have similar backgrounds, they are likely to agree with him. For Moore all good things were good in virtue of their having the simple (intuitively apprehended) quality *good*. But is *good* a simple quality? Might it not be better to compare it with *coloured* rather than with *yellow*? For perhaps just as there are different colours, although all give us a characteristic visual sensation, so there are different forms of goodness, all arousing a characteristic sensation of moral approbation. Thus we can imagine a set of cushions, objects that all have *colour* but are of different colours; likewise we can imagine a variety of actions and people that are good but good in different ways: a kind action, a loyal friend, a merciful deed, an unselfish person. It *may* be that the underlying 'good' is the same, but it is by no means self-evident.

We need to consider another objection relating to Hare's view of the supervenient character of *good* (see chapter IV, page 31). We may say 'This is yellow' or 'This is coloured' and consider something else that is the same *except* for being not-yellow or a different colour. But if we say 'This is good' can there be something else that is exactly the same *except* for being not good? Although we may talk of *good* as an abstract quality it is intrinsically bound up with *what* is good, i.e. with what Moore called *the good*. 'Yellowness' or any colour has a meaning and a significance on its own, but without any substantive 'good', like 'pleasure' (see page 47), seems to disappear. We can also object to Moore's view (part of his argument against equating goodness with some other (natural) quality) that, for instance, 'reflecting light of a certain wavelength' is not what we *mean* by 'yellow', and 'always gives pleasure' is not what we *mean* by 'good'. It is true that 'yellow' and 'good' have a meaning and significance independent of the descriptions so that it makes sense to ask, 'Does light of this certain wavelength appear yellow?' and 'Is pleasure good?'; but, if we believe that the questions should be answered affirmatively, then our concepts of yellow and good are thereby affected. Then 'yellow' *does* acquire more significance than that of being a visual sensation and 'good' *does* mean more than arousing moral approbation. We have to recognise goodness and yellowness as qualities of certain entities but, having found out more about those qualities, our concepts are clearer and perhaps more profound. These criticisms must lead us at least to question Moore's view that goodness is a non-natural quality. If kindness, happiness and pleasure in actions, situations and persons is observable why not goodness? Goodness is an intrinsic part of a kind action, so can we draw a firm line between natural (observable by the senses) and non-natural (not observable) qualities? As we saw in chapter III, it is very difficult, perhaps impossible, to separate observable fact from value and Moore himself has been criticised for implicitly relying on perception when he wrote about 'seeing' goodness.

But whether good is a non-natural or a natural quality is of no real importance; for the naturalistic fallacy, if fallacy it is, lies in attempting to define the indefinable, or to analyse the unanalysable. That is why it is just as futile to define (or analyse) the natural quality yellow (or coloured) as it is to attempt to define (or analyse) the non-natural quality good. Indeed Moore himself acknowledges this when he says, of *good*, 'Even if it were a natural object, that would not alter the nature of the fallacy nor diminish its importance one whit. . . . I do not care about the name: what I care about is the fallacy.'[11] Of course the fallacy is a fallacy only if we think that *good* is distinguishable from *the good*. If we think that *good* (the quality) can only be understood in relation to actions, persons and situations then there is no fallacy and discussion of it will, at best, merely serve to remind us that we are capable of making moral evaluations and that this, though related to the capacity for making factual judgments, is a different capacity. As was stated at the beginning of this chapter, Moore is generally regarded as an intuitionist but, since judgments about what he called *the good* do involve appeal to observable consequences, he has something in common with consequentialists. If we do not accept his strict separation between *good* and *the good* his position seems even nearer to the consequentialist assessment. However, that separation was very important for Moore; intuitive apprehension of *good* was, for him, the core of ethical judgment.

Other twentieth-century philosophers have developed Moore's views and have tended to view the notions of duty and obligation as basic. They believe that moral discourse refers to objective properties and that these properties are known because we have a natural capacity to make moral judgments. Like all intuitionists Moore and his followers claim that moral judgments are statements that can be intuitively apprehended as being true or false. However, as Moore frankly admitted, there is no way of *proving* that an ethical judgment is true or false. He conceded that intuition might mislead but he clearly implied that careful reflection would guide to a correct intuition just as careful observation would guide to a correct factual description and that therefore we would agree on ethical judgments. Here lies the danger of intuitionism for, since intuitionists are not content with a subjective view, that is they do not think that ethical judgments are *merely* personal opinions, they will hold that anyone who disagrees with their judgment is guilty of moral blindness or wilful perversity. This was put very clearly by Samuel Clarke, writing in the eighteenth century:

> These things are so notoriously plain and self-evident, that nothing but the extremest stupidity of mind, corruption of manners or perversity of spirit can possibly make any man entertain the least doubt concerning them. For a man endued with Reason to deny the truth of these things, is the very same

thing as if a man who has the use of his sight should, at the same time that he beholds the sun, deny that there is any such thing as light in the world; or as if a man that understands geometry or arithmetic, should deny the most obvious and known proportions of lines and numbers, and perversely contend that the whole is not equal to all its parts.[12]

And 'tis as absurd and blameworthy to mistake negligently plain right and wrong . . . as it would be absurd and ridiculous for a man in arithmetical matters ignorantly to believe that twice two is not equal to four or wilfully and obstinately to contend against his own clear knowledge, that the whole is not equal to all its parts.[13]

Ethics is concerned with the basis of moral judgments. Phrases such as 'moral consciousness' and 'apprehension of moral qualities' imply that we can make these judgments but, if intuitionists are correct, there is no criterion of truth apart from appeal to moral intuition. Intuitionists point out that judgments of visual fields have, as their ultimate criterion of truth, what we see, the visual sense impression. As we read in chapter II, it is simply the case that most people do agree about the nature of what they see, and differences of opinion can be resolved. By contrast deep moral disagreements may not be resolved. Does it then follow that there are irreducible differences of moral vision, or could there be some other reason for such differences? Would it be possible to find a rational resolution of differences, or at least a rational basis for discussion, and yet still appeal to moral values, values perhaps intuitively apprehended but justified by something more than intuition?

If we do not wish to appeal to divine inspiration or guidance, it is necessary to look for some characteristic(s) of human beings that would involve moral behaviour. Since morality is concerned with behaviour towards others what we seek must be a feature of human societies, and moreover of *all* human societies for we hope to find moral values that are universally accepted. I suggest that there are two universally accepted moral principles: keeping trust and benevolence. They are not to be taken as principles external to human nature, principles *imposed*, but as principles of behaviour that have developed from pragmatic rules to moral laws as human societies developed. I suggest that keeping trust is a fundamental and necessary requirement for the very existence of human society – there is honour even among thieves – because no society can cohere if the members have no reliance on one another. I also hope to show that benevolence (taken as the regard for the welfare of at least some others apart from oneself) is also necessary. We have not, as is patently evident, developed so as to behave *invariably* in a trust-worthy and altruistic way: we are egotistical, selfish and all of us can be cruel. I suggest that it is our awareness of the conflict between immediate self-interest and the interests of others that makes us aware of morality; we do not have to appeal to a conflict between an autonomous and heteronomous will as Kant did.

The moral principle of keeping trust is the fulfilling of obligations (explicit and implicit), doing one's duty; it also carries with it the principle of acting justly (fairly). In the next chapter I shall show how particular obligations and duties come to be accepted as a matter of course in a particular society, but what is to be stressed here is that there is *always* an accepted code of justice and fair dealing in any human society.[14] The codes vary but the underlying moral principle is that of keeping trust. Particular obligations arise from the customs established by the particular society; one is expected to behave in certain ways in certain situations and this may be as a result of formal laws and contracts or of less formal conventions. The *moral* force of an obligation rests on the moral principle of keeping trust.

The Oxford philosopher John Austin (1910–1960) – not the jurist referred to by Hart at the beginning of chapter XI – said that certain words got their impact from their negatives; he called them 'trouser words' because they were unusual in that the negative (not the positive) 'wore the trousers' and determined the significance of the word. Austin took the word 'real' to be a trouser word since he argued that it got its impact by implicit contrast with what was not real in a given context. Thus a real duck might be *real* as opposed to a toy duck, or it might be *real* as opposed to a stuffed duck, or it might be *real* as compared with another bird something like a duck but not actually a duck.[15] Similarly when we say that someone has a duty we imply that it is *wrong* for him or her *not* to undertake that duty: perhaps because society expects it, or, in another context, because there was a promise, or contract. The moral force of the obligation rests on the moral reason that would make it wrong *not* to fulfil that obligation.

To fulfil a customary obligation is, of course, to act rightly, but often it is what is expected and does not thereby earn any special commendation. Only in relatively unusual circumstances, the fulfilment of some rather onerous duty, perhaps incurred through the negligence of some other person, is such an action regarded as being worthy of special moral approbation. In general we expect a trust to be kept, promises to be honoured, obligations to be fulfilled, duties to be performed and dealings to be fair. This is perhaps a trifle naive; few human beings fulfil all their obligations, and we do accord special respect to those who show themselves consistently trustworthy, reliable and just, but we expect reasonable conformity to the principle by most people most of the time. Society could not work unless trust was usually kept and that is why there is strong condemnation for those who *break* trust; the condemnation against transgressors is far greater than is the praise for those who conform. There is a close relationship between 'wrong' in the moral sense and 'illegal', for laws, for all their faults, do represent and are usually supported by moral codes. Formal laws are intended to enforce compliance with what are held to be acceptable codes of behaviour; just because they are formal they are rarely able to accommodate the moral nuances of particular situations but despite their faults, the basic support they have is, and must be, moral support.[16] In both sophisticated and primitive societies there are many unwritten laws, well-known but unformulated codes of behaviour and moral conventions. The primary purpose of these informal rules is also to guide people to conform to what the group takes to be right behaviour. Because they are informal, unwritten laws may be more adaptable and more useful. However it is also possible for custom to be more onerous than formal laws and established customs are invariably harder to alter than formal laws. Unwritten laws of, say, the duties of parents to children can be adapted to suit circumstances but they may also condone petty tyranny. Whether good or bad (in the sense that they do or do not support basic trusts), legal penalties are exacted if we fail to fulfil, or renege on, formal obligations; social penalties are exacted if we flout unwritten laws and customary codes of behaviour.

We have a natural capacity to make moral judgments and are, by nature, morally aware but we do not first become aware of a basic principle, keeping trust say, and *then* embody it in a moral code; rather we learn the content of morality from the codes of behaviour we observe; it is the sophisticated who appreciate that the codes of their own society are not, in themselves, *basic* moral principles. Hence the intuition that we have at first, by which we recognise *the good*, and *good* is profoundly influenced by our social (usually including religious) codes.

It is worth stressing that the force of obligation is moral, not merely prudential; it is just the case that human beings are like this and it is because they are morally aware that there is such a subject as ethics. As Anthony O'Hear says:

> certain facts about human psychology and about human activities provide a basis for at least a limited application of such virtues as sympathy, justice, truthfulness and courage. If these facts were different, if human beings generally lacked moral feelings and if they never shared projects, it is possible that nothing we regard as morality would have any role in human life.[17]

O'Hear continues by suggesting that this contingent fact about human nature gives us a basis for objective values:

> The approach to morality I am suggesting here does not appeal to any divine perspective or superhuman telos.[18] It is based entirely on a combination of human nature, human tradition and human choice, although it is worth stressing that a type of objectivity is secured in this approach by stressing that neither nature nor tradition is entirely plastic.[19]

The view that morality is based on fundamental and intuitively accepted principles is not incompatible with the belief that knowledge of these principles is a divine gift, and perhaps some of the aversion to the acceptance of the existence of objective (and therefore absolute) moral principles stems from fear of religious superstition. But although absolutism is not incompatible with certain religious beliefs, there is no reason to suppose that human moral sense is necessarily a gift bestowed by God. Even less necessary is it to believe that our notion of what is good is simply what God decrees to be good. As stated at the beginning of this chapter, both Christian and pagan thinkers have, in the main, held that 'the good', or holiness, or moral worth are not made so as a result of divine approbation; rather God (or the gods) have been deemed to value goodness because it is worthy of approbation. In the passage below Plato argues that that which is loved by the gods (the god-beloved) is not the same as that which is good (holy). The holy is indeed loved by the gods because it is *worthy* to be loved, but it is not made holy by virtue of this divine love.

> SOCRATES . . . we agree, do we not, that the holy is loved because it is holy, rather than it is holy because it is loved?. . . Also that what is god-beloved is god-beloved because it is loved by gods, that is by reason of this love. . . . For the one is beloved in virtue of being loved, whereas the other is loved because it is worthy to be loved.[20]

Like many animals, we live in social groups, and though, as implied above (page 66), co-operative behaviour is not necessarily a sign of moral behaviour, it would seem that co-operation must increase the chances of individual and of species survival. However, the case for altrusim developing by natural selection meets the objection that natural selection is not a selection of species but of the genes carried by individuals, and if one individual member of a species has genes making it more altruistic than others it is *less* likely to survive. Thus though the whole species would benefit if the members put the interests of others before their own, it would seem that the appropriate genes would be unlikely to spread. The point is made by Peter Singer:

> . . . any genes that lead to altruism will normally lose out, in competition between members of the *same* species, to genes that lead to more selfish behaviour, before the altruistic genes could spread through the species as a whole in its competition with *other* species.[21]

Singer points out that there are analogous examples of animal behaviour, behaviour that seems altruistic and would put the individual at a disadvantage, which present the same difficulty. How is it possible to explain, by appeal to evolution by natural selection, the warning call given by an individual blackbird at the approach of predators (for the bird that warns would single itself out for attack), or dolphins staying to help a wounded dolphin (instead of making their escape), and so on?

Singer argues that natural selection is not based on the survival of the genes of an individual, although of course she must live long enough to reproduce, but on the survival of those genes in her descendants. Hence those individuals that show altruism in respect of their young and near relations (i.e. those with whom they have a considerable number of genes in common) will indeed promote the continuance of altruistic characterising genes, because the individuals so favoured will have an advantage over others who are not benefiting from altruism. In time the 'altruist genes' would spread through the community, for in early times human societies were small and the members would have been blood relatives. So the original kin altruism would develop into group ultruism, and both can be accounted for by appeal to natural selection. If individuals are self-aware, the genetic promotion of group altruism will be reinforced because human beings (and perhaps some other animals with memories) may be expected to show gratitude and to reciprocate past services; thus reciprocal altruism will support and be supported by genetically based altruism. So, the objection to the suggestion that altruism evolved by natural selection can be met: even though natural selection selects individual genes, the net result can be to give an evolutionary advantage to a species whose individual members are guided, at least to some extent, by concern for the interests of their young, of their kin and of their group.

An evolutionary account of morality can also show that morality differs from mere prudence. Firstly, as we have seen, moral individuals have to be aware of themselves as agents. Mackie points out that not only does purposive behaviour depend on individuals having the concept of their personal identity, but also that we assume self-awareness when we explain actions that promote the well-being of the agent:

> Someone can have a reason, then, for doing what will lead or is likely to lead, or even is wrongly believed by him to be likely to lead to the satisfaction, perhaps in the remote future, of some desire (etc.) that he now has. . . . Can we say that he now has a (prudential) reason for an action which will tend to satisfy not any desire which he now has, not even a present desire that his future desires should be fulfilled but only a desire which he knows he will have later? We can indeed say that he has such a reason. . . . But in saying this we are leaning on our concept of the identity of a person through time and the associated expectation that a human being will behave as a fairly coherent purposive unit over time, that his purposes at different times will

agree with one another fairly well. Human beings are more likely to flourish if they show such purposive coherence over time, so that it is not surprising that we have this useful cluster of concepts and expectations. . . . Our established concept of personal identity through time is here functioning analogously to an institution like promising, introducing a requirement for attention to the future well-being of what will be the same human being as the agent in question.[22]

Mackie treats moral behaviour as prudential behaviour, i.e. behaviour that is motivated by egotism rather than consideration of the interests of others. We may remember that Singer argued that genuine altruism probably started with care for offspring and near relatives (likely to have many genes in common), so that the 'altruist genes' were thereby selected. Mackie says that even a genuine concern for the interests of others is, at the last, a very enlightened policy of general (including the individual's) interest so that what is moral is also the (prudentially) best policy;[23] morality becomes *more* prudent than prudence:

> . . . almost everyone should, in his own interest, welcome the fact that there is . . . some system of morality. . . . But this does not completely resolve the tension. It leaves unanswered the question 'Why should I not at the same time profit from the moral system but evade it? Why should I not encourage others to be moral and take advantage of the fact that they are, but myself avoid fulfilling moral requirements. . . ?' It is not an adequate answer to this question to point out that one is not likely to be able to get away with such evasions for long. There will be at least some occasions when one can do so with impunity and even without detection. Then why not? . . . In the choice of actions moral reasons and prudential ones will not always coincide. Rather the point of morality . . . is that it is necessary for the well-being of people in general that they should act to some extent in ways that they cannot see to be (egotistically) prudential and also in ways that in fact are not prudential. Morality has the function of checking what would be the natural result of prudence alone.[24]

This paradoxical position is a consequence of taking the well-being of humanity as the ultimate goal; behaviour so motivated is altruistic by definition and it will indeed serve to check personal (egotistical) prudence. Nevertheless it can be described as (prudentially) best for humanity. Mackie goes on to point out that because nearly all of us have moral feelings our conscience will tend to make us feel uncomfortable if we act immorally, and so conscience converts what is an altruistic action into a prudential action:

> . . . our concept of personal identity through time itself functions as a sort of institution, aided by a contingent present desire for one's own future welfare. We can, then, fall back on the comparable fact that nearly all of us do have moral feelings and do tend to think in characteristically moral ways, and that these help to determine our real interests and well-being. Why we are like this is in the first place a psychological question . . . but more fundamentally it is a sociological and biological question to be answered . . . by an evolutionary explanation. If someone . . . has at least fairly strong moral tendencies, the prudential course, for him, will almost certainly coincide with what he sees as the moral one, simply because he will have to live with his conscience. What *is* prudent is then not the same as what would be prudent if he did not have moral feelings.[25]

It is to be noted that Mackie is not saying that we are moral as a matter or policy, in the sense discussed in chapter I, but because we want to *be* moral in order to live with our consciences. It is simply part of the nature of most human beings to be like this and so the prudence to which Mackie alluded is not prudence in the ordinary sense; as stated above it can be regarded as another expression for altruism for it is part of what is (prudentially) best for humanity. Thus, even if it is taken as being ultimately prudential, morality transcends ordinary egotistical prudence.

We have analogous examples of transcendence of capacities which have evolved and have transcended their original function of helping survival: our powers of sense perception, of ratiocination, and of speech are all involved in our capacity for aesthetic response. There have been philosophers and poets who have believed that our moral sense is closely related to our aesthetic sense and even that morality and love of beauty are closely connected. This is implicit in Moore's belief that beauty was of the good (had the quality of goodness). Keats says:

72

'Beauty is truth, truth beauty,' – that is all
Ye know on earth, and all ye need to know.[26]

The relationship between morality and art, in that moral values
need to be justified by the artist, is considered by Bertrand Russell.
Russell does not hesitate to acknowledge the existence of evil and it
is interesting to note that, although he was an atheist, he refers to
God when discussing morality and the moral sense. Nevertheless he
treats morality as a secular matter and links the moral sense to the
aesthetic sense. He has this in common with Keats, but he differs
from Keats in giving more weight to the intellect for he thinks that
intellectual, aesthetic and moral capacities develop together in each
person. He takes beauty to be an end in itself; he also acknowledges
that scientific knowledge can be sought as an end in itself but he
thinks that the ends of the artist can best arouse and develop our
delight in human life. Here Russell shows himself to be a secular
humanist; for Russell morality is a means of eliminating evil and
therefore a means of improving the quality of human life. The
following extracts come from letters written to Robert Nichols in
1925. From the letter of 17 June:

> I hesitate to advise you about reading, or about the kind of
> abstract ideas, to which, as an artist, you should give life. . . . I
> think Man, in our day, is too proud, but men (in relation to the
> mass of other men) are too humble. Both effects come from
> science via industrialism. Blake says 'humble to God, haughty to
> Man', but nowadays we are the other way round.
>   . . . the scientist is concerned only with knowledge, which is
> valuable chiefly as a means. As an end it has some value, but
> only as one among ends. As ends, the artist's ends seem to me
> better. . . . It is clear that to commend an ethic successfully,
> artistic gifts are required; but that is outside the value of art as
> such. . . . I think delight in life and the world is the ultimate
> good of man, or at least part of it, but that as our mental powers
> develop delight has to have more and more mental content if it
> is to be satisfying and not evanescent. It seems to me that the
> artist supplies the means of continuing to feel delight in spite of
> expanding mental power. Mental power seems also good in
> itself, and is the business of the scientist. The moralist has a
> different function, dependent on the existence of evil, and
> therefore not concerned directly with ends but with means. I

doubt whether the moralist ever does good unless he quickens people's sense of the value of ends; but to do this a man must be an artist.[27]

From the letter of 5 November:

I do not believe there is any 'why', or that the word 'means' anything at all. I agree with Satan in the Tentation de Saint Antoine. But I do not find that I lose the capacity for happiness or for feeling life worth while. The point is this: Human life may have significance, through human desires, though Nature at large has none. When you suggest that the artist creates significance, I agree: he creates human significance, even when he thinks he discovers cosmic significance. I want man to be more lordly, and less afraid of asserting himself against an indifferent universe. I think all values are human, but none the less important on that account.[28]

Although our moral sense cannot be shown to depend on a divine benefactor or on any religious belief, Russell's writing shows how much moral writing of avowed and firm non-believers is permeated by religious and mystical ideas. In addition, it cannot be denied that all major religions are concerned with morality. Though moral sense is not divine, it is closely involved with the human tendency to appeal to suprahuman powers. Eric Dodds has suggested that religion grows out of the individual's appreciation of her relationship to the *total* environment (the natural world: mountains and rivers, plants and animals, and people) and that morality grows out of the individual's awareness of other people with aspirations and needs.[29] Dodds considers that religion and morals were at first independent and that in primitive societies, such as the society of Homeric Greece, the highest good was not the enjoyment of a quiet conscience (that which leads to Mackie to argue that the moral may become the prudential act, see above, page 72), but the enjoyment of public esteem. The moral force rested solely on the respect and esteem of *other* people, and so it was only wrong to do something that actually did incur public censure. A deed could not be immoral if it were not discovered! As we saw in our earlier discussion, the question 'Why should I not profit from the moral system but evade it?' (see Mackie, quote 24, page 71) can be countered, though for us unsatisfactorily, by 'Why not, so long as I am not found out?'.

Primitive societies may have had such a moral code; that is the moral climate of what Dodds calls the shame culture. He says, 'In such a society, anything which exposes a man to the contempt or ridicule of his fellows, which causes him to "lose face", is felt as unbearable.'[30]

With the development of religious beliefs, that is belief in a God (or gods) personally interested in human affairs, there arises the belief that any wrongdoing would be observed by God (or the gods) even if not by other ordinary human beings. Thus Shakespeare gives the following lines to the king, Claudius, in *Hamlet*:

In the corrupted currents of this world
Offence's gilded hand may shove by justice,
And oft 'tis seen the wicked prize itself
Buys out the law: but 'tis not so above;
There is no shuffling, there the action lies
In his true nature, and we ourselves compell'd
Even to the teeth and forehead of our faults
To give in evidence.[31]

The quote from Lord Devlin at the beginning of this chapter shows that the interaction and indeed interdependence of morality and religion are acknowledged today. Devlin continues by saying that the very validity of moral codes depends on religious belief. This is not to contradict Dodd's account, for it can be argued that the non-religious shame culture is not truly moral and, as we have seen, Dodds thought that inner awareness and inner censure of moral transgression (guilt) developed with religion. It may be a contingent fact that human moral awareness developed with religious faith or, and one suspects that Devlin would favour the alternative, it may be that religious faith is necessary for there to be a private and a social morality. It remains an open question whether we need some kind of belief in a Deity concerned with the way we behave to sustain our moral sense or to allow it to develop. An evolutionary account of the emergence of moral principles can be compatible with a secular morality but it does not require that religious faith should play no part. Religious faith, some would call it superstition, is characteristic of all but the most primitive societies and it may be more necessary for the maintenance of moral behaviour than many people think.

At all events, people do now understand that an act can be wrong, morally wrong, although never discovered by others; the notion of

75

guilt, as opposed to shame, is quite independent of discovery or proof of that guilt. Perhaps, at first, guilt was connected with fear of detection by God (or gods), but later, and certainly in our own time, it is associated with self-censure, with an unquiet conscience. For conscience is simply self-acknowledgment of wrongdoing and as Mackie has said (see above) the threat of the discomfort produced by an unquiet conscience is a powerful internal sanction for most of us; for some it may be more powerful than censure by their fellows, for others the public shame may be more potent than inner unease. We shall consider the influence of private guilt shame further when we discuss the relation between morality and the law in chapter XI.

The capacity to understand a moral code can be compared with the capacity to learn a language; there are an enormous number of different languages spoken by human beings and also an enormous number of different moral codes of behaviour. Yet differences of moral principles (as opposed to codes of behaviour adapted for different societies), and the moral values related to them, are considerably less than differences between the languages of different societies. This is because the conditions necessary for human beings to live together in harmony are relatively constant, whereas there is no environmental or cultural or psychological reason for languages to be alike. As Quine says:

> Moral values may be expected to vary less radically than
> language from one society to another, even when the societies
> are isolated. True, there are societies whose bans and licences
> boggle our imaginations. But we can expect a common core,
> since the most basic problems of societies are bound to run to
> type. Morality touches the common lot of mankind as the
> particularities of sound and syntax do not.[32]

Finnis makes the same point:

> Students of ethics and of human cultures very commonly
> assume that cultures manifest preferences, motivations, and
> evaluations so wide and chaotic in their variety that no values or
> practical principles can be said to be self-evident to human
> beings, since no value or practical principle is recognised in all
> times and all places . . . But those philosophers who have
> recently sought to test this assumption, by surveying the
> anthropological literature . . . have found with striking
> unanimity that this assumption is unwarranted.[33]

He proceeds to elaborate secondary principles such as condemnation of murder and restriction of sexual activity, that he regards as moral principles common to all human societies. I am inclined to the view that Finnis develops this over-much, and that many of his examples of universal values, e.g. the value of human life, have to be so heavily qualified that they become void of content. However, his basic thesis, that all human societies have moral values and that human beings have a moral sense, remains established.

Quine suggests that moral values are analogous to scientific theories but he argues that scientific theories are more objective than moral principles since the former are supported by appeal to what *is*, outside in the world, and scientific theories can be judged to be true in the sense that they correspond* to observable events and entities that are independent of the theory. By contrast moral principles and values must be judged by observable moral acts and these moral acts are given moral significance by the very principles that they are called on to support. Thus the principles cannot be justified by appealing to something independent of themselves and so can only be judged for coherence.

> The empirical foothold of scientific theory is in the predictable observable event; that of a moral code is in the observable moral act. But whereas we can test a prediction against the independent course of nature, we can judge the morality of an act only by our moral standards themselves. Science, thanks to its links with observation, retains some title to a correspondence theory of truth; but a coherence theory is evidently the lot of ethics.[34]

Nevertheless Quine admits that ultimate moral ends do in fact command considerable agreement because, as we have seen, he says that the basic problems of human societies are very much alike. In another essay he hesitates in claiming that science must yield an objective truth, i.e. independent of human culture. We must, he says, admit the possibility of the existence of a culture with an entirely different kind of science guided by different norms (perhaps due to a different way of organising sense experiences).

> Might another culture, another species, take a radically different line of scientific development, guided by norms that differ sharply from ours but that are justified by their scientific

findings as ours are by ours? And might these people predict as successfully and thrive as well as we? Yes, I think that we must admit this possibility in principle; that we must admit it even from the point of view of our own science, which is the only point I can offer. I should be surprised to see this possibility realised, but I cannot picture a disproof.[35]

Thus Quine concedes that empirical knowledge rests on norms which are implicit in our theories and scientific knowledge, like moral principles, must ultimately be judged by a coherence theory of truth.

There is no scale of moral rectitude and 'That was the right thing to do' cannot be supported by appeal to some pointer indicating rightness on a scale. But there is a difference between 'It seems to me that that was the right thing to do' and 'That was the right thing to do', analogous to 'That paper looks red to me' and 'That paper is red'. The analogy is brought out more clearly if we compare apparently inconsistent judgements of the type considered in chapter II; for example 'That paper looks red but it is really white' with 'That seems right but it is really wrong'. As we saw, such inconsistencies are only apparent because two different languages, that of 'seems' and 'is', are being used in the judgments.

In general we do not think that a person who makes a sincere judgment that a piece of paper is red (when it is really white) is mistaken because she lacks the capacity to judge colour. We may infer that recent experiences have temporarily distorted her judgment (she might just have removed green-tinted glasses, for example), or that not enough attention was paid to relevant circumstances (the paper may have been illuminated by red light) or, in the case of more complex judgments, that there were expectations and/or a tendency to favour a particular scientific theory. Likewise, in relation to a sincere moral judgment that an action is right (when it is really wrong), we do not necessarily think that the faulty judgment shows moral blindness. Recent experiences, failure to be aware of relevant circumstances and a tendency to favour particular kinds of action can affect the judgment. The situation is more complicated, and it is therefore easier to be mistaken in moral judgment, but the parallel is there.

However the analogy is not exact for two reasons; firstly the parallel between the empirical and the moral judgment can seem strained. Compare 'This paper looks red to me though I know it 'is white' with 'This seems right to me though I know it is wrong'. The latter judgment, as a *sincere* judgment, is odd, if not, strictly speaking, illogical. We do not think that the former judgment is odd because we are familiar with perceptual mistakes and illusions and well used to the double language of 'seems' and 'is' in this context. But when we make sincere moral judgments it is assumed that we have already allowed for circumstances and are asserting what we (at least) think *is*. Thus the explicit contrast between 'seems' and 'is' is generally out of place in a moral judgment. However it is not totally redundant for unless we are very stubborn, we can be persuaded *afterwards* that we had made a mistake and that what had seemed right was not; and so 'That seemed right to me but now I know it was wrong' is not odd – though such admissions are not commonly made!

The second reason for questioning the analogy is that the seems/is distinction of empirical judgments may not be thought to be the same as the seems/is distinction of moral judgments just because there is no measurement or scale of rectitude. However I think the analogy does hold and it may be seen to hold by comparing a pre-thermometer judgment of 'This seems hot to me' and 'This is hot' with 'This seems right to me' and 'This is right'. Even before temperature could be measured it would have been reasonable to distinguish the subjective personal reaction from an assessment that was independent of any particular individual. The distinction is clearer if objective measurement is possible, but it can be made even if measurement is impossible.

Thus the analogy stands, though it has to be admitted as a matter of plain fact that it is difficult, even when the circumstances are not in dispute, to get the unequivocal agreement on moral judgments that we expect, and usually get, on empirical judgments. Or perhaps this is only how it appears on first consideration? We think of those empirical judgments concerned with the matching of a pointer on a scale, judgments that command universal agreement, and compare them with, for example, a judgment as to the morality of corporal punishment. It is unlikely that *any* judgment on this topic will command universal agreement – different groups of people will make different evaluations. Indeed, though it is unlikely, it would not be impossible that a lone individual could make a moral judgment that no one else supported and yet, elsewhere and elsewhen, that one 'eccentric' would be thought to be right. The judgment made by the son of the cannibal chief in 'Eating people is wrong' is an example. But I suggest that we need to analyse the judgments more carefully. The moral equivalent to a simple pointer reading is judgment on the validity of a basic principle and just as the significance of the pointer reading requires further assessment, so the moral judgment has to be assessed in a practical situation. Then, moral judgments on less fundamental matters than those of principle, such as the morality of corporal punishment or of eating people, are analogous to empirical judgments on established theories, say the explanation of the sun's movement. Just as there can be disagreements on matters of empirical fact once we leave the most simple observations, so there can be disagreements on matters of moral value once we leave the most basic principles. Moral disagreements often *seem* to be basic disagreements to the protagonists because they, like all of us, learn to apply their moral capacity on the basis of the moral culture around them (see page 67) and what is regarded as embodying and fulfilling obligations of trust and as showing benevolence will depend on the conventions established where they grow up. Thus people from different cultures may believe that their moral disagreements are more fundamental than in fact they are.

VII

CONVENTIONS OF TRUST AND INSTITUTIONAL FACTS

Since what constitutes keeping trust is closely related to the particular social customs and conventions of each society, and since these can be very different, the kind of behaviour that is morally required will be different in different societies. What is regarded as a duty and an obligation must depend largely on conventions, the currently accepted codes of behaviour, because these give rise to expectations as to what people will do. In any stable society people rely on their expectations being fulfilled and mutual moral duty arises as a result of this reliance. For example it is universally acknowledged that parents have a duty of trust, an obligation to care for their infant children. This is to be expected since, as we saw in chapter VI, it is probable that altruistic behaviour evolved from genes of caring parents being inherited by their offspring. In most human societies[1] it is taken for granted that parents shall protect their infant children and cater for their needs; any parents who fail to do this will be morally condemned. But the *kind* of care that parents are expected to give depends on the social codes of their society.

In certain Polynesian societies many services that we should take to be parental duties are customarily performed by aunts and uncles. In Ancient Greece weak or deformed infants (and sometimes healthy female infants) were left to die on hillsides; it is interesting to note that the Ancient Greeks were reluctant to kill the babies directly – had this been the custom Oedipus would not have survived to fulfil the prophecy and Paris would not have lived to elope with Helen and so set off the train of events leading to the fall of Troy. In Ancient Greece and in some other societies it was accepted that parents should offer their children as sacrifices to the

81

gods; we may remember that Abraham was prepared to sacrifice his son Isaac to Jehovah. These practices may seem bizarre, barbaric and immoral to us because we have different social codes, but the societies concerned have not rejected the moral principle of keeping trust nor even the principle that parents have moral obligations to children. It is the concrete nature of that obligation and also what other duties ought (morally) to override it that are assessed differently, and so vary greatly, in different societies.

It must be stressed that to be aware of different social codes, and to acknowledge that members of different societies take their particular codes as being supported by the same basic moral principle, is not to condone all codes that would be to indulge in moral relativism. There are two types of ground for condemnation: firstly we may think that a practice is not in fact justified in the way that the practitioners believe it to be, for example we may think that Abraham was simply mistaken in believing that any higher power required him to sacrifice his son. This objection is not a moral objection, it is based on factual considerations; in the case of Abraham the objection would be that we can find no evidence to support a belief that the sacrifice of Isaac or indeed any human sacrifice would benefit Abraham himself or his people. Secondly we may object on moral grounds, contending that the practitioners have failed in moral reasoning and that the behaviour condoned or encouraged violates an important principle derived from the principles of trust (or benevolence) and that the violation is not justified. Thus we might contend that even if human sacrifice *did* produce beneficial consequences for society these were not sufficient justification. It might be argued that *no* social benefit could justify human sacrifice. It is this type of objection, a moral objection, that gives rise to moral argument and to genuine moral conflict. I referred to conflict in discussing Forster's judgment in chapter III and we shall be discussing the problem in more detail in chapter IX, but it is worth pursuing the particular conflict involved in the clash of personal and social obligations.

Let us take a problem from Ancient Greece, and since we are concerned only with moral issues, we will consider the conflict without questioning the factual belief that it was necessary to have the help of the gods and that this help could be obtained with human sacrifice. The story of the sacrifice of Iphigenia by her stepfather Agamemnon, so that the Greeks could get a fair wind from the gods and so set sail for Troy, is a story of a moral dilemma that was regarded as such at the time. Agamemnon thought it was wrong to kill her, for he had undertaken the parental duty of care (she was his stepdaughter), but he also had a duty to avenge his brother Menelaus. Should he propitiate the gods, thereby allowing the ships to sail and avenging his brother's honour, or should he place the interests of the child higher? He hesitated, and whilst he hesitated the seas remained calm, there was no wind for the ships. Finally he decided to sacrifice Iphigenia, and, by subterfuge, got her to be brought by his wife (the girl's mother), Clytemnestra. He was sure that Clytemnestra would oppose the sacrifice, and indeed she did; she thought that it should not happen. Her judgment was no doubt affected by the fact that Iphigenia was her daughter, but her objection was on moral grounds: protection of a child was more important than protection of a brother's honour.

Such problems are not the problems only of primitive societies, bedevilled by superstition. The power of the Greek legends lies in their appeal to emotions and moral difficulties which are always with us. At all times there can be moral conflict between personal obligations and public duties. Thus Lovelace's lines in the seventeenth century:

> Tell me not (Sweet) I am unkind,
> That from the nunnery
> Of thy chaste breast, and quiet mind,
> To war and arms I fly.

> True; a new mistress now I chase,
> The first foe in the field;
> And with a stronger faith embrace
> A sword, a horse, a shield.

> Yet this inconstancy is such,
> As you too shall adore;
> I could not love thee (Dear) so much,
> Lov'd I not honour more.[2]

The potential conflict between our duties to society and our duty to individuals is with us today.

The existence of moral conflicts, and the fact that different people take different views as to how they should be resolved, does not undermine the universality of the principle of keeping trust.

Trust is implicit in the codes of all human societies and generally the duties and obligations arising from accepted codes of behaviour carry greater force than do duties incurred by law or through formal contracts. The point is made forcefully in Shakespeare's *Macbeth*, in the scene where Macbeth is contemplating the murder of Duncan:

> He's here in double trust
> First as I am his kinsman and his subject
> Strong both against the deed; then as his host
> Who should against his murderer shut the door
> Not bear the knife myself.[3]

Macbeth is not concerned with the law; he is concerned with his *moral* obligations as he and his fellows understand them. Our moral feelings of what we ought or ought not to do are intimately bound up with social customs and codes: we have a duty to our kinsmen, to our rightful monarch (in Macbeth's and Shakespeare's time this was a religious as well as a secular duty), and to those whom we invite into our house. The duties are there today partly embodied in laws, and also part of expected behaviour. They were very much stronger in Shakespeare's time and earlier for in medieval societies the duty of care of a host would demand that, morally, he must not harm anyone, even an enemy, who took shelter under his roof. We see this in Wagner's *Die Walküre*, when Siegmund takes refuge in Hunding's house. On discovering that Siegmund is an enemy, Hunding will not harm him whilst he is in the house; he says:

> I was called to vengeance
> to make amends
> for family blood.
> I came too late
> and, now returning home,
> the tracks of the villain who fled
> I discover in my own house.
>
> My house will shelter
> you, Wolf-cub, for today.
> For this night I put you up.
> But with stout weapons
> arm yourself tomorrow.
> I choose the day for fighting.
> You must pay for those deaths.[4]

That there are accepted social customs and codes of behaviour, giving rise to expectations and therefore to moral obligations, is more than a contingent fact. For because it is universally the case, it is a conceptual fact, in that part of our concept of a human society is a society where there are duties and obligations.

Because we are as we are there are certain things that we say and do that entail moral obligation. J.R. Searle discusses the moral aspect of making promises in our society;[5] he says that the fact that a promise is made entails a moral duty to fulfil that promise. The making of a promise is an *institutional fact* in that if a person promises to do something, this is a fact that puts him or her under a moral obligation to act as promised. Thus the moral obligation, what a person *ought* to do, is derived from a fact, the fact that a promise was made. Similarly the fact that we implicitly accept a certain code of care for our children means that we acknowledge, as a matter of fact, that we have duties to our children and therefore that we *ought* to behave in certain ways.

Now it is true that to use the words 'I promise' sincerely and seriously is to accept the moral code such that saying, 'I promise to do X' is equivalent to saying 'I place myself under an obligation to do X'; therefore the fact of promising entails 'I *ought* to keep my promise by behaving in an appropriate way'. Searle argues that a moral 'ought' is thus derived from a factual 'is'; that is, that statement of fact, a statement about what is the case, can entail a statement of moral value, that is a judgment (a moral judgment) about what (morally) ought to be done. But this is not so, because though it is a fact that the promise has been made (or that society expects a certain standard of care for children), that fact *includes* the moral directive. Searle recognises the special nature of the fact of promising by calling it an institutional fact. The institution is part of a social code of duty, a code which is accepted by the individual and by society (the institution). Therefore a moral 'ought' is derived from the moral 'ought' that is an essential part of the promise; it is an 'ought' which is acknowledged implicitly when the promise is made. Similarly most parents accept (generally implicitly) a moral responsibility for the care of their infant children. The few who do not accept this code ignore the fact that society regards them as having moral obligations; it is an institutional fact that parents *ought* to care for their infant children and so we can derive from the fact that a person has an infant child the moral 'ought', namely that she *ought* to look after it. This example shows, perhaps more clearly than the example of promising, that the moral 'ought' is built into the situation because our society usually implicitly (but if necessary explicitly) upholds certain kinds of behaviour as being morally and sometimes legally obligatory. There are many other institutional facts, facts that carry obligations with them. In our society borrowing is an institutional fact because it carries with it a moral obligation to return what is borrowed. The signing of a cheque is an institutional fact because it carries a moral (as well as a legal) duty to know that the cheque will be honoured by the bank. The fact that two people get married, that is the process of marrying, is an institutional fact since they then have certain moral as well as legal obligations. This last example shows that the moral obligations carried by institutional facts are dependent on the current moral code of the institution (society), for the obligations incurred by marrying in Britain today are markedly different from those incurred by the people who married in the nineteenth century. A hundred years ago marriage in Britain was undertaken as a union for life and entailed sharing of property (with the husband having absolute control) and commitment to sexual fidelity. Divorce was legally difficult, though easier for a man than his wife, and those who were divorced (both male and female) were ostracised by a considerable part of society. Today very few would take this attitude to marital obligations; even those who held that it was morally right to be faithful would be chary of outright condemnation of those who had a different moral view of sexual relations. Thus the significance of the word 'marriage' has changed along with the nature of the institutional fact that it embodies.

As we become aware of the use of such words as 'promise', 'borrow', 'marry' and so on we learn, at the same time, the duties and obligations that are expected of us as members of our society. These words are not value-laden as described in chapter III, they are obligation-laden. The moral *value* lies in fulfilling the expected obligation but the meaning of these words refers to the nature of the obligations. Thus if it were not uncommon for people to break promises, the word 'promise' would not carry moral force; indeed if a child grows up with adults who regularly fail to keep their word, the child will not take promises seriously. Mackie[6] takes the child's word 'bags' as a word acquiring moral force through its use. 'I bag that' implies 'I have a right to that' by those who accept the moral code of bagging. But for those who do not accept the code, no right has been established and the announcement 'I bag that' is then equivalent to 'I want that'. Language is the tool of thought but thought is also dependent on language because through using language we develop our concepts and our knowledge about the world and about ourselves. Through language we increase our capacity for logical reasoning and we also develop our moral concepts and our ability to make moral evaluations. Our concept of the basic moral principle of keeping trust is strengthened not only through the use of words such as 'promise', 'borrow', 'marry' and so on, in situations where certain obligations are incurred, but also by the tacit acknowledgment of their implications as to how people *ought* to behave. Obligations to keep promises, to repay debts and to remain faithful in marriage are based on secondary principles and social values that are part of the moral code of a society. These principles will be discussed at length in chapter X but we have already seen that different societies have very different codes. However all codes of behaviour carry obligations and also implicitly (if not explicitly)·appeal to what is held to be fair dealing (justice).

Different societies have different concepts of justice: different concepts of distributive justice (fair shares) and commutative justice (fair dealings between individuals and groups of individuals). Codes of behaviour considered just by a society may be established by custom and/or through formal laws. We shall be considering the role of morality in the law in chapter XI; here we need only point out that customs and formal laws generate expectations, and hence justice under the law is the social aspect of keeping trust. The behaviour that is considered just is, of course, different in different societies: There are great differences in laws of fair distribution of goods relating to inheritance, marriage, rewards for work done and so on; there are differences in laws of penalties to be exacted if agreements are not honoured or debts not repaid. The concepts of distributive and commutative justice can thus appear very different even though they all rest on a moral principle of fulfilling expectations and so keeping trust.

In many societies there are subcultures whose members respect codes of behaviour that are different from the codes of the principal culture. For example there are groups in late-twentieth-century Britain who think that it is morally wrong to eat animal flesh; others who think that it is morally wrong to hunt animals; there are

Jehovah's Witnesses who think that it is morally wrong to receive or to give blood transfusions, and there are people who think it right for elections to be held without a secret ballot. The moral obligations of the members of sub-groups therefore differ from the generally accepted moral obligations in society at large. On the whole, their behaviour in relation to others *in their sub-group* is tolerated; but toleration does not generally extend to allowing them to require others outside the sub-group to conform. The situation is not always so simple and sub-group values can bring about complex moral problems: should a Jehovah's Witness be allowed to prevent her child from having a blood transfusion? Should people who object to hunting be allowed to interfere with those who do hunt and, if so, to what extent? In chapter XI we shall be discussing the interaction of the law and social values and also the possible justification for breaking the law for what are seen as moral reasons. Here we need only note that the moral obligations within a subculture may differ markedly from those of the main group and yet all are held to depend on the principle of keeping trust.

The special moral obligations within a subculture are to be distinguished from behaviour of members of a group that the main group would call a criminal culture. Although, as indicated in chapter VI, it seems that there is some honour among thieves (because there could not be a cohesive social 'underworld' without a degree of trust), it is also true that the vast majority of criminals are aware that they are not keeping trust with their fellow citizens, for apart from those criminals who are insane or psychopathic they know that they are disregarding the normal social obligations. They will seek to avoid detection and discovery – in this they are very different from those who are convinced of their own moral rectitude (say the CND protesters) and who act openly to try to change the accepted morality. If criminals are caught they may admit a 'fair cop' and plead guilty, or they may try to justify their actions by some kind of Robin Hood defence (in this case they are appealing to higher duties, see chapter IX), or they may seek to mitigate censure by pleading difficult circumstances, to do with their upbringing or their current situation. But whatever the reaction when apprehended, the basic principle of trust, of social obligation, is not questioned.

Thus examples of bizarre moral codes of a subculture, or of another society are not counter-examples to the universal acceptance of the principle of keeping trust; they are examples of the different ways in which that principle is implemented. Whether it be Ancient Greece, the African jungle, medieval Europe or twentieth-century Britain the notions of duty, of obligations towards others, keeping faith and behaving honourably were and are morally important. They are directly related to the fundamental principle of keeping trust. The codes and conventions vary, the principle does not. We should note that codes change over time; what was regarded as an important trust (say the duty of a host) may become less important; what was regarded as of negligible importance (say duty of care to a servant or employee) may become very important.

Changing circumstances, such as those brought about by technical advances, increased psychological knowledge of human nature, changing religious beliefs and changing opinions of what is fair shares and what is proper reward, will alter moral judgments on social values and codes of behaviour. The judgments change because the behaviour is seen as being differently related to the principles of keeping trust. For example, it has been established that a significant minority of people are homosexual and that no harm is done to society if homosexuality is practised with restrictions analogous to[7] the practice of heterosexuality. There is an implied duty of care, and therefore of moral obligation, in both homosexual and heterosexual relations; the duty is greater in the latter because of the possibility of conception, and therefore of a third person being involved.[8] Non-moral circumstances affect codes of behaviour because they affect our notions of where duty and honour lie.

Thus the view that there are universal values does not entail that any particular code of conduct must be absolutely and permanently morally 'right' or 'wrong'. The *justification* of any moral code, however, must always be by showing how it is related to the basic principles. They *do* remain unchanged.

VIII

BENEVOLENCE: MAN AND BEAST

The two basic moral principles proposed in chapter VI were those of keeping trust and benevolence, though it was pointed out that they were not completely independent. For example, the question 'Ought we to help others in distress?' is an appeal perhaps to duty rather than to kindness. Are there not, then, occasions when we have a *duty* to be benevolent? We must also recognise that, though there can be sensible debate as to whether we ever have a moral obligation to be benevolent as well as sensible debate on obligations in particular circumstances, there is no doubt that we have a general duty not to be malevolent. (We shall be considering this negative aspect of benevolence later in the chapter, in our discussion of the moral issues involved in the treatment of animals.) Thus it could be argued that there is only one fundamental and ultimate principle – keeping trust – and that benevolence should be regarded as the negative of malevolence so that it could be treated as part of the duty. However, although the distinction between keeping trust (duty and obligation) and benevolence cannot be clear-cut, there are so many examples of actions that merit praise because they transcend what is normally taken as duty that it is probably more helpful to consider benevolence as a separate moral principle. To be benevolent is to show an active concern for the interests of others, more than is required or even expected by one's fellows. We can show benevolence to people to whom we have no obligations and to creatures who do not have rights.

We have seen that in any society the moral code tells people that they have special duties towards some others involving them in obligations that are not due to all members of the society. So, in

Britain, if a dependent relative or a close friend is in financial distress we are deemed to have a moral duty to help (possibly also a legal duty). The greater the dependence and/or the closer the friendship, the stronger is the moral obligation. But if a stranger asks for our help, perhaps begging in the street or writing after our win of a football pool prize is announced, we do not have a moral duty to give anything. Assuming the applicant is not starving (and even then we may decide to call the police) we shall not have failed in a *duty* if we refuse help. Depending on the circumstances, on our past experiences, and perhaps on other obligations we have, we may or may not feel some moral inclination to be charitable. It may or may not be the case that others will consider us to be mean to ignore an appeal, just as those who fail to contribute to established and organised charities may be thought to be mean; but no one is going to accuse us of immorality. Those who do give money to strangers may be praised for benevolence though, in certain circumstances, they could be held to be gullible rather than benevolent – a soft touch.

A relatively trivial but illuminating example of changes in attitude to what is regarded as a duty or as an act of benevolence is provided by changes in attitude to the custom of 'tipping' in a restaurant and hotel or to servants in a private house. Until relatively recently people in the catering industry and private domestic servants were poorly paid and the tip was an understood part of their emoluments. Hence it was a moral duty to tip, and any person who did not tip the expected 10 per cent would, unless service had been exceptionally poor, have failed in an implicit obligation. Today many restaurants and hotels charge for service so that the gratuity has become part of the bill and is explicitly required. In these circumstances, any further payment shows benevolence, perhaps a token of appreciation of especially good service, for there is no moral duty to give more. Tipping in restaurants where there is no service charge, or of servants in private houses, remains a minor obligation but, even in these cases, the moral requirement is not as great as formerly since wages can now be expected to be adequate. Indeed tipping, as an act of benevolence, is not welcomed by all; objectors to tipping hold that work well done should be paid for as of right, not as a charity and not even as an implicit social duty. They argue that the practice of tipping tends to keep regular wages artificially low and also that it is degrading for workers to have to depend on benevolence, even a benevolence that is more accurately described as a moral obligation. This is part of a general contempt for charity; charity, it is said, panders to the pride and self-importance of the donor and to the obsequiousness of the receiver so that both are demeaned.

However those who are the potential beneficiaries of tipping do not always take this view, as the writer of the letter below makes plain:

From Mr A. Ross
Sir. Surely the merits of a standard, agreed and advertised taxi tariff, which takes into account the running costs of a cab, are self-evident.

Mr Pearce's tariff reform (August 27), Suggesting a free-for-all on pricing, would bear hard on people who use occasional taxis because they cannot afford to run a car: Glasgow has significantly more taxis per head of the population than Edinburgh. It would also prove expensive for those who have no alternative means of transport – e.g., at a provincial airport late on Saturday night.

Tipping for services, real or imagined has always been the hallmark of a civilised person. High-principled people – I will not say *Guardian* readers – like Mr Pearce may object to the 'odious practice', but what he is really suggesting is that he incorporates a compulsory tip (the 'tout compris', as we say), in the form of a higher fare structure.

The abolition of tipping would remove one of the few amusements of the driver's life, the gratuity assessment he makes on each hire. Whether it be the bare fare of certain races and sexes, the hidden bare fare (10p on a £10 hire) of mortgaged suburbia, the cigarette-and-conversation tip substitute, or if, on the other hand, the gratuity is princely, or even gentlemanly, we accept gratefully whatever is offered.

After all, taxi drivers talk, provide local information and carry baggage, as may be necessary. We expect nothing, but we do not reject gratuities. Mr Pearce should realise that 'tis not in taxi drivers to command gratuities. We must deserve them.
Yours faithfully,
A. ROSS, Secretary,
Edinburgh Airport Taxi Association,
Edinburgh Airport, Edinburgh[1]

For many of us the word 'charity' has unwelcome overtones; as we saw in chapter III, values change with time and, since fact and value are to some extent interdependent, a change in values produces a modification of fact. But in earlier times the word 'charity' signified a virtue of high moral value – St Paul held it to be the most noble of all:

> Though I speak with the tongues of men and of angels, and have not charity, I am become as sounding brass or a tinkling cymbal.
> And though I have the gift of prophecy, and understand all mysteries, and all knowledge; and though I have all faith, so that I could remove mountains, and have not charity, I am nothing.
> And though I bestow all my goods to feed the poor, and though I give my body to be burned, and have not charity, it profiteth me nothing.
> Charity suffereth long, and is kind; charity envieth not; charity vaunteth not itself, and is not puffed up. . . .
> Rejoiceth not in iniquity but rejoiceth in truth.[2]

We may note that St Paul distinguishes charity (a genuine love and concern for others) from the mere distributing of largesse, and even ranks it above martyrdom.

Shakespeare praises mercy, an important form of charity:

> The quality of mercy is not strain'd,
> It droppeth as the gentle rain from heaven
> Upon the place beneath: it is twice blest;
> It blesseth him that gives, and him that takes.[3]

The original view of the charity, benevolence and mercy would have had no place for a condescending Lady Bountiful giving soup and pennies to the lower orders, nor for a patronising diner bestowing money on ill-paid waiters. True charity is to give generously and without pomp, but we have to bear in mind that in St Paul's time, and in Shakespeare's time and, indeed, very much later, there would have been no questioning of a social order that accepted as inevitable vast differences between the fortunate and the needy. Current social objections to charity are that it helps to support a society that still tolerates far too great a difference between rich and poor and is, therefore, basically unjust. If we take this seriously then scope for private generosity is clearly much restricted.

Tipping and the morality of tipping are a small part of two wide moral questions: firstly, do acts of benevolence (individual or state benevolence) actually impede the establishment of better conditions for the less fortunate, and secondly, will the moral impulse to be kind, generous and merciful be subdued if society is organised so that the needy are provided for, and all are justly treated? In Britain today we have special arrangements to help the poor; they can claim what is called 'supplementary benefit'. Unlike the various state pensions that are financed by contributions from pay and are due as of right, supplementary benefit is given as of right only to those who can show hardship. This payment represents public as opposed to private charity.

There are social reformers who object to the system of supplementary benefits as much as they would object to private charity, on the grounds that it supports a system that they think is unjust and immoral. Others offer less radical objections; they object to the system as administered because they say that it is inefficient: those who could claim relief are not always aware that they are eligible or are too proud to ask for it. This is analogous to the objections to private charity based on the grounds that it is too haphazard. But, in the main, objections centre on the former view, that charity bolsters up an unfair system and prevents social progress.

Discussion of the extent to which the state (and therefore the taxpayer) has a moral duty to help the less fortunate must be based on what is to be taken as *hardship*[4] and on whether the ignoring of hardship is morally indefensible.[5] It is sometimes claimed that any inequality is immoral so that if anyone has less than anyone else that in itself is hardship and an immoral situation. More commonly there is moral argument on whether there should be a limit on the extent of inequalities. Moral discussion is also about the possibility that individual impulses to be generous and benevolent are discouraged by Welfare State taxation. Such a discussion is about moral behaviour rather than moral principles, for it is concerned with what does happen rather than with what ought to happen. In general we must consider that benevolence, a basic moral principle, is to be encouraged; it is a matter of observable fact whether it is or is not encouraged in a Welfare State. It does seem that today well-to-do people give less money to worthy causes than they did in the nineteenth century but this may be at least partly a result of the

decline of religion (and formal church charities) and a decline in the
relative opulence of the well-to-do. The part played by state action is
not clear, nor whether less generous behaviour is due to a decline in
the feeling of 'liberal guilt' that profoundly affected the fortunate in
the early years of the twentieth century.

Singer's view that our moral behaviour and moral awareness
evolved by natural selection was discussed in chapter VI. There we
saw that the evolution of altruism would come about through care
for offspring, kin and neighbours. A later extension to strangers can
be expected but it is unlikely that we shall ever have the same
concern for them as we have for those close to us; it can indeed be
argued that it would be *immoral* not to have particular regard for
the family for whom we have special responsibilities. Nevertheless
we are aware that all human beings have rights and that all have
obligations to others.[6] Relatively recently we have also come to
believe that there is a moral duty to have at least some concern for
the interests of animals, a *moral* concern that is to be contrasted
with the prudential concern of the farmer or stockbreeder.

There are very great differences of opinion as to the *moral*
concern we should have for animals even if we confine ourselves to
the diverse opinions in late-twentieth-century Britain. Most people
are prepared to eat animals and to wear clothes made from fur and
leather, but there are a growing number who think that this is
immoral; a majority of the population still tolerate the current
methods of factory farming but a substantial minority think that this
should be more strictly controlled; probably about half the population enjoys or tolerates hunting, shooting and fishing and about half
find these activities morally obnoxious (in varying degrees); the
majority of people oppose painful experiments on animals except-
ing those that seem necessary for medical research. Practically
everyone opposes ill-treating animals for 'fun' or as a result of
neglect and there are already quite strict laws and regulations
concerning experimental procedures. Cruelty, whether through
indifference and lack of care or deliberate, is punishable by law and
certain 'sports', bull-baiting, cock-fighting and hare-coursing are
now legally prohibited.

It is salutary to learn what was thought to be acceptable behaviour at other times and in other places; the following two
quotations describe eighteenth-century Ethiopian customs:

Shortly after leaving the ruins, Bruce came upon three men
driving a cow before them. They had black goatskins upon their
shoulders, lances and shields in their hands and appeared to be
soldiers. Suddenly they tripped up the cow which fell heavily to
the ground. One of the men sat across her neck, holding her
head down by the horns; another twisted a halter about her
forefeet; while a third, with a knife in his hand, jumped astride
her belly and then, to Bruce's 'utter astonishment', cut out two
huge hunks of flesh from her flank which were placed upon a
shield. While the cow was still held down, the flap of skin was
replaced over the gaping wound and fixed in place by small
skewers. 'Whether they had put anything under the skin, I
know not,' wrote Bruce; 'but at the river side they prepared a
cataplasm of clay with which they covered the wound. Then
they forced the animal to rise, and drove it before them to
furnish them with a further meal.[7]

Bruce's description of an Ethiopian banquet does, however,
give a clear impression of what some of these parties must have
been like. . . .

A cow was then brought to the door and its feet tied. Its
throat was then cut slightly to let a few drops of blood fall upon
the ground in satisfaction of the Mosaic law. Two butchers then
cut the skin along the spine and placing their fingers between
the skin and flesh of the animal, flayed it alive. All the flesh of
the buttocks was first cut off in solid, square pieces; and the
prodigious noise the animal made was the signal for the
company to take their places. . . .

When the hunks of meat were brought in, 'the motion of the
fibres yet perfectly distinct', the men cut it up into steaks while
the women sliced it into smaller pieces. . . .

Other wads of bread and flesh so quickly followed the first
mouthfuls that the men, leaning over the table, were in constant
danger of being choked. Their hunger at last satisfied, they
performed the same service for the women. . . . Men and
women all drank together out of big handsome horns, while the
last remaining slabs of tender flesh were being hacked from the
cow outside, still alive and bellowing in agony.[8]

Practices in England could also be barbaric. The extract from
Precious Bane, an early twentieth-century novel about village life a

hundred years earlier, shows how people at the beginning of the nineteenth century regarded bull-baiting:

'Chaps, I've come to ask ye to stop this.'

There was a long bepuzzled silence. Then Huglet laughed and slapped his thigh, and roared again. Grimble looked at his boots and gave a snigger.

'Well, that's a good un!' shouted Huglet. 'Stop the bull-baiting, oot, young fellow?'

'Ah. I'd lief stop it.'

'And what for would you stop it, dear 'eart?' asked Grimble in a soft, sing-song voice.

'Stop it?' roars Huglet, 'he *canna* stop it.'

'I'd lief it was stopped over all England.'

'You'd lief a deal, young man. Why, I tell ye there's bin bull-baiting in England ever since it *was* England! Take away the good old sport and it wouldna *be* England!'

All this he said in the same loud roaring voice.

'I asked ye, what for would ye stop it?' repeated Grimble, soft and obstinate.

'Because, it's a cruel, miserable business.'

'It inna cruel. The dawgs like it. They enjoy it. And bull likes it right well.' . . .

'What's it matter if they enjoy it or not? I enjoy it!' says Huglet. 'That's enough, inna it?' . . .

'Ah!' says the landlord of the *Mug of Cider*, 'I've heard tell of folks as wanted to stop the long keeling. I've even heard of tithree as wanted to stop wars and rumours of wars, but bull-baiting? Never in life! Whoever, save a few fratchety parsons, did ever want to stop a baiting?'

'He must be going a bit simple, poor fellow,' says Grimble.

'Feel well, weaver?' . . .

'I wunna be robbed of my sport!' he said. . . . 'We want our sport, I tell ye!'

All the men with dogs looked black and muttered –

'Ah, that's righteous! That's gospel! We want our sport!'[9]

The extract is interesting because it shows that the arguments used to support the bull-baiting are the same as arguments used to support other sports that are tolerated still today: it's an English sport and England wouldn't be England without it; we've always had it; it isn't cruel; the animals like it; anyway *we* like it. It does not follow that because we take the arguments as unconvincing in the context of bull-baiting they would have no force for supporting other sports, but it is clear that they cannot be regarded as conclusive in their own right. Why is it that today we do forbid at least some 'sports', sports that were tolerated and enjoyed by decent ordinary people only a few decades ago? I suggest it is because beliefs about the nature of animals had been fundamentally changed by Darwinian evolutionary theory.[10] Before Darwin there were learned and kindly men who thought that animals were mere machines without any thoughts or conscious desires; they could not feel pain. Descartes, Wren and Boyle had this opinion and though we may be inclined to conclude that this gives evidence for the view that the learned can lack common sense it is true to say that most people did not think of animal pain as being a matter for moral debate. Everyone thought that human beings were fundamentally different from animals; people were *not* a kind of animal, they were made in God's image and had immortal souls. The animals had been put into the world by God so that human beings could use and enjoy them. Even after the publication of *The Origin of Species* in 1859, there was serious speculation about animals' capacity to feel pain. We cannot be logically certain that animals suffer as we do, indeed we cannot logically prove that other people have inner experiences like our own. Our firm belief that they do is based on observation of their behaviour and it is further supported by the fact that all human beings have very similar nervous systems. Likewise our beliefs about the feelings of animals is based on observation of *their* behaviour and knowledge that many animals have a nervous system that is similar to the human nervous system. Thomas Henry Huxley, writing in 1874, considered it highly probable that animals had inner experiences and held that we had a moral obligation to treat them as if they were capable of experiencing pain:

> But though I do not think that Descartes' hypothesis can be
> positively refuted, I am not disposed to accept it. . . . We know,
> that, in individual man, consciousness grows from a dim
> glimmer to its full light, whether we consider the infant
> advancing in years, or the adult emerging from slumber and
> swoon. We know, further, that the lower animals possess,
> though less developed, that part of the brain which we have

98

every reason to believe to be the organ of consciousness in man; and, as in other cases, function and organ are proportional, so we have a right to conclude it is with the brain; and that the brutes, though they may not possess our intensity of consciousness, and though from the absence of language, they can have no trains of thoughts, but only trains of feelings, yet have a consciousness which, more or less distinctly, foreshadows our own.

I confess that, in view of the struggle for existence which goes on in the animal world, and of the frightful quantity of pain with which it must be accompanied, I should be glad if the probabilities were in favour of Descartes' hypothesis; but, on the other hand, considering the terrible practical consequences to domestic animals which might ensue from any error on our part, it is as well to err on the right side, if we err at all, and deal with them as weaker brethren, who are bound, like the rest of us, to pay their toll for living, and suffer what is needful for the general good.[11]

Today the view that animals are proper objects of moral concern and that they ought to be treated as autonomous individuals with rights analogous to those of human beings has not inconsiderable support. Just as eighteenth-century social reformers argued for the Rights of Man and asserted that the poor were entitled to the same consideration as the rich, so present-day campaigners for animals argue for Animal Rights. The problem of whether animals do have rights, analogous to human rights, is a difficult one to solve. It is worth considering because if animals have rights then we have duties towards them. I am inclined to oppose this and to say that animals do not have rights because *they* do not have moral duties. Individuals who have rights are entitled to certain benefits but they also have explicit and implicit obligations and duties to others which they acknowledge to be duties. Thus individuals with rights must be individuals who are, in general,[12] morally aware. It may be that some animals are morally aware, especially as regards their own species, but the evidence is not very strong. It is certainly the case that there are many species of animal that undoubtedly have interests and who give no sign of being morally aware.

But if we rely on the moral principle of benevolence then we can make a moral appeal to human beings, asking them to respect the interests of animals *as a matter of charity*. Here 'charity' signifies more than 'love of humanity'; it means 'love of living creatures' and so it has become extended beyond the original biblical sense.

An argument against evaluating our behaviour to animals in terms of benevolence is that, if we follow the analysis at the beginning of this chapter, it would seem that though we should praise those who are kind to animals we would not censure those who fail to be kind. Failure to keep trust, on the other hand, is condemned. Perhaps mere failure to be kind is morally neutral but we are concerned with positive cruelty. It was shown in chapter VI that though fulfilling obligations does not merit special praise, undertaking a particularly onerous duty does. Likewise though failure to be benevolent does not attract moral censure, positive unkindness, cruelty, does. Benevolence merits praise, lack of benevolence is neutral, malevolence attracts censure. Hence we do not have to get involved in the difficulties of animals' rights in order to establish the moral point that *it is wrong to be cruel to animals*. We shall praise those who are especially kind: rescuing the drowning dog, feeding the birds in winter, taking in a stray cat, etc., and we shall censure those who are cruel: keeping animals in bad conditions, failure to feed, unnecessary experiments, and so on. The many problems as to how we ought (morally) to behave towards and to treat animals are not hereby solved but discussion may be more profitable if it is based on appeal to the general moral principle of showing benevolence (and refraining from malevolence) to all creatures that have interests.

Different opinions about the extent of our responsibilities are *not* differences about the value of the moral principle of benevolence (or of duty, if we think that animals have rights); they are differences arising from different opinions as to the relative importance of animal interests as compared with human interests – just how far are animals to be treated as persons?[13] Thus in the extract quoted below the writer acknowledges the immorality of cruelty to animals and also the duty of preserving species from extinction, but does not think that the majority of human beings (public opinion) supports the view that animals are entitled to consideration comparable to the consideration we accord (or believe we ought to accord) to members of the species *homo sapiens*. There is little doubt that the writer is correct – attitudes to animals have changed but most people do not believe that animals (even the most 'advanced' species) merit the same moral concern as do human beings. *In this respect* debate about the treatment of animals is analogous to debate about abortion and embryo experimentation where the status of the potential person is in question. (See also chapter X, page 117 *et seq.*)

SEALS OF DISAPPROVAL

The ministers are asked by the Commission, at the behest of the European Parliament, to approve a regulation prohibiting the importation into the EEC of seal products from Canada and Norway. . . .

The sponsors of prohibition point to the cruelty inseparable from the slaughter, by clubbing, of nearly 200,000 seal pups on the Atlantic coast of Canada this year. They point to the triviality of the end product of the trade – après-ski boots, key ring pendants, cigar cases and other such frippery, and, grimmest mockery, toy baby seals fabricated from the pelts of slaughtered baby seals. The cruelty they describe is thus shown up to be unjustified by utility or any worthwhile ulterior purpose. . .

One might have no difficulty, when exposed to the argument, in deciding one's own attitude to artefacts made out of that material. The question however is not one of private attitude but public policy. Is there to be statutory prohibition of the trade? There is an initial presumption against interfering in trade – the general welfare is best served by an open system. . . .

Under what might be called the existing rules the case for banning seal products is not made out. . . .

In the matter of cruelty, the comparison of the way seals are killed with the way other creatures are hunted or culled in the wild is not so unfavourable to the sealers as to justify their special classification. Anyone who ponders the question should ask himself whether his feelings would be so strong if the little creatures were not furry but scaly, their eyes not large and dewy but small and malevolent in appearance. . . .

Hitherto the rules have been drawn from two basic propositions: man has the power and right to make use of animals for his benefit, eating them, working them, wearing them, by hunting or domestication or husbandry; and in exercising that right he must avoid wanton cruelty, and (a newer idea) he should not exploit any species to the point of extinction.

It is now proposed that that embodies an immoral attitude towards man's relation to the rest of the animal kingdom; that he has no licence to exploit animals at his pleasure and convenience; and that they have 'rights' analogous to those men have come to accord to each other; that of any treatment to ask 'would you do it to your fellow men?' is relevant. This view of the matter has made a lot of ground very rapidly. It has the force of a popular movement. It is a focus of protest. But the ministers in Brussels tomorrow should not mistake it for dominant public opinion.[14]

How does the moral principle of benevolence stand in relation to the principle of keeping trust? Can we rate one as higher than the other? To show benevolence is, as we have seen, to go beyond the duties required by society, and we do tend to rate generosity arising from a spontaneous sympathy for others as being not only more endearing but somehow morally superior to just fulfilling obligations; the latter seems to make moral behaviour a matter of austere calculation.

I hesitate to endorse this view. We have already seen that there is no strict distinction between duty and charity and that what one person, or indeed what society, might take to be benevolence could be regarded as a duty by others. For example it is generally regarded as benevolent or charitable to give money to Oxfam but some people think that they have a *duty* to help starving people overseas. Now it seems extraordinary to maintain that people who decide, perhaps after hearing an appeal, to give money to Oxfam, are morally superior to those who, after prior deliberation, have decided that it was their duty to give. Rather these people could be held to be more conscious of morality and have a deeper sense of moral awareness; their love of humanity (and other creatures) may be just as great as the love shown by the spontaneous giver. The notion that benevolence is somehow morally more meritorious than duty is connected with the fact that benevolence is, as we have seen, to do more than duty requires. But this is to confuse human warmth, an endearing but non-moral characteristic, with a genuine concern for the interest of others.

A genuine concern for the interests of others is shown both in acts of duty *and* in acts of kindness; the former are explicitly or implicitly required by society and contribute to social cohesion; the latter may be required by the conscience of the individual or may be a result of natural sympathy for others. The fact that there can be no sharp distinction between duty and kindness also supports the view that neither moral principle is more important or is to be rated as morally higher.

A conflict of moral principles is a true moral conflict and, as we shall see in the next chapter, there can be conflicts of duty and benevolence, conflicts of duties, and conflicts of potential acts of benevolence. But many so-called moral conflicts do not involve conflicts of basic moral principles but conflicts involving assessment and interpretation of *facts*; they may also involve differences of opinion as to what the facts are. In chapter IV (page 28) it was stated that Ayer held that all ethical debate was about matters of fact, and though I do not suggest that *all* such debate is really about fact, a very great deal of it is. As indicated above (page 100) differences about the morality of treating animals as sources of food, as subjects for experiments, etc. arise as a result of differences about the relative weights of human and animal interests that themselves are a consequence of different views as to the 'personhood' of animals. It has also been pointed out (page 98) that our moral attitude to animals has been greatly altered by science – the facts have changed. Not that the position of facts is simple, for, as we saw in chapter III, fact and evaluation are interdependent and it is very difficult, perhaps impossible, to separate the issues of fact and value. This is why ethical debate is so complex and moral conflicts are confused with factual differences. Even if we grant that the two basic moral principles are not questioned there will be debate as to how social conventions are guided by them, and to what extent; and there will be debate on whether other principles are or are not validly derived from them. There may be irreducible differences of opinion when there is conflict at basic level. Moral discussion cannot always resolve conflict but we may hope that it can clarify issues.

IX

MORAL CONFLICT AND RATIONAL CHOICE

There are three kinds of moral conflict:
(1) conflicts of obligation and benevolence, when to do one's duty or to act justly may involve unkindness;
(2) conflicts of obligation, when it is not possible to fulfil one moral obligation without failing to fulfil another;
(3) conflicts of benevolence, where kindness or particular attention to one person precludes like kindness to another.

The last type of conflict, conflict of benevolence, is not, of course, a conflict involving moral *obligation*, for we take all acts of benevolence to be moral actions that go beyond the call of duty. Nevertheless there are situations where competing appeals to our charitable natures pose a problem which we may see as a moral problem. A classic example is the problem facing a person who sees two strangers drowning and who is able to rescue only one of them, and that at great risk. Who should she pick? The one seen first, the one who is calling, the man, the woman, the younger, the elder, and so on? There are many factors that could affect the decision, but agonising as the decision may be, the choice made is not truly a moral choice and there is no *moral* conflict. The morality lies in trying to rescue at all; an individual will not be blamed for rescuing one rather than the other. Indeed, except that such a serious situation cannot be viewed lightly, the rescuer might make a choice for a frivolous reason: I chose the one with red hair.

This is apparent if we consider a less grave clash: it may be that a person can afford to give a handsome present to one friend, something which the friend would be truly delighted to receive, or to give several pleasant small presents to several friends. If no friend is in need the choice can be made entirely by reference to the inclinations of the donor. An analogous situation confronts most of us in giving to recognised charities: to give a large amount to only one or less to several.

Of course the reason why we tend to think that the choice involves a moral decision is that it is very very rare that the beneficiaries, be they drowning people, friends or charities, are so alike that there is no moral element in the choice. This does not mean that there is a clear-cut solution to these problems in practice for, as we shall see, there can be different moral factors, inclining to different choices. But it does mean that it is possible to justify a choice, in almost all circumstances, by appeal to something more than plain fact, and certainly to something more than a whim. Thus we might decide to rescue a child rather than a woman or a woman rather than a man because it was more likely that we would be successful in saving the smaller person and we take it to be *morally* better to rescue some person than to fail to rescue another. On the other hand we might decide to rescue a woman rather than a child because it was possible that the woman was a mother with family responsibilities, and so on. Analogous moral reasons could affect our choice of action in giving to friends or to charities. Thus the conflict that arises when there are conflicts of benevolence are moral conflicts when a choice is made for moral reasons. If alternative choices also have moral support, considered to be as strong, or nearly as strong, as that which is actually made, the moral conflict is the more acute.

An example of a type of situation where duty and benevolence may conflict, and so indicate different courses of action, is that confronting a doctor treating a patient with a fatal illness. The doctor has a duty to tell the patient the truth, namely that death is almost certain to come soon, but benevolence may incline her to say nothing, possibly to allow the patient to entertain spurious hopes. We all know that different doctors decide in opposing ways and that the same doctor may take a different decision with different patients. Different circumstances clearly justify different decisions but, even after we have allowed for these, there remains an element of subjective preference in the moral choice an individual makes. So, even when the facts of the situation, and the likely consequences of each choice, are agreed (and it is difficult to get that far!), there can remain a possibility of disagreement as to the morally best way to act. Different people may still make different choices and the same person may make a different choice, in what are acknowledged to be morally similar circumstances, at different times. We have to accept that human beings are not completely rational and not completely and dispassionately consistent. The lack of consistency is particularly apparent in ethical (and aesthetic) judgments, that is in value judgments, though it is not very difficult to find inconsistencies in other judgments, empirical, logical and metaphysical. But ethical judgments are particularly likely to be inconsistent, and it is probable that they also have an irreducible 'core' of subjectivity that remains after full allowance has been made for the delicate complexities of the human situations that are subject to such judgments. I suggest that the core is irreducible because the character of the judge (or judges) is *part of* the situation: we do not and cannot completely remove ourselves from a situation that calls for our moral evaluation – we feature as one of the factors influencing our own assessment. However, having accepted the existence of this 'core' and having acknowledged that the judge is part of the situation judged, we are not forced to conclude that ethical judgments are necessarily *totally* subjective, and certainly not forced to conclude that they are not subject to rational criticism. All we need to acknowledge is that there is not necessarily just one correct judgment in any situation; there may be several or there may be none.

A consequence of this is that there will be occasions when we will respect the moral decision of someone who has made a different choice from the one that we made, or would have made, in the same circumstances. This is not to say that we will respect *any* sincerely given moral judgment, but rather to say that we do not *necessarily* think that someone who takes a different view of a moral problem must be immoral or morally blind. In this chapter I shall defend the proposal that two or more people who make different moral choices, each sincerely believing that she has chosen for the (morally) best, may yet consider that the (different) choice of others is also a moral and rational choice.

Those who differ may have a moral discussion about their choices and may, or may not, change their opinion about their own choices. It is important to stress that it *is* possible to have a dispute about moral values even though it is unlikely to be a 'purely moral' dispute because facts and values are, as we saw in chapter III, so interdependent. But, as was stated in chapter VIII, I am rejecting the position taken by Ayer in *Language*, *Truth* and *Logic*, that we *never* argue about ethical values.[1] We may of course believe that our disputant is mistaken about the facts of the case or about the agent's motives and we may believe that if these were cleared up then we should have agreement on the moral issue. We may believe that the consequences of a course of action have been wrongly estimated and that if *that* were put right there would be agreement. But I suggest that there can be differences of *moral* assessment and that rational argument, followed by agreement, to agree or to disagree, is possible. Nevertheless I do accept that Ayer is right in saying, 'argument is possible on moral questions only if some system of values is presupposed.'[2] I differ from him because I think that having accepted the *fundamental* moral principles, there can be further argument about values that are derived from the fundamental principles. Such argument is essentially moral argument.

Rational moral argument is not possible unless the two fundamental principles of keeping trust and showing benevolence are accepted and it is the case that morality itself consists in respect for those principles, so that one who questioned them could not be a moral being. Acceptance of the moral principles is analogous to disputants in a factual argument all accepting that there are physical objects (entities known through sense perception but which continue to exist independently of any perceiver) and to accepting that there are causal relations between physical objects, or to disputants in a logical discussion accepting the validity of standard inferences such as *modus ponens*[*3] and *modus tollens*.[*] Factual debate would be impossible without some common ground for there can be no *dis*agreement if there is absolutely no agreement; logical discussion and argument would be impossible if the very framework of logical thought was not accepted. Likewise ethical and moral discussion and argument can arise only from an agreed basis of what morality *is*. So we can disregard the exceptional individual who lacks perceptual powers, or who cannot appreciate the force of logical necessity in a conclusion derived by valid inference, or who cannot understand the moral force of the basic moral principles.

As was stated at the end of chapter VIII, the complexity of moral debate is partly a result of the difficulty of dealing with issues involving an interdependence of fact and value. In addition there is a problem with terms that have a direct moral import. These do not

107

demand specialised knowledge, they are familiar: 'good', 'bad', 'right' and 'wrong' appear to present no problem and everyone thinks that she can enter into moral debate without appreciating that such terms are highly emotive. We saw in chapter IV that for Ayer the only significance they have (when used normatively) is as terms to rouse emotion and, even if we think they also have a genuine moral function, their emotive power cannot be ignored and must be allowed for if rational moral debate is our aim. Lastly it is almost impossible to make general moral rules, apart from the rules implied by the fundamental principles. This is because not only is the nature of each evaluator a relevant factor but also because a very slight change in the external empirical circumstance can profoundly change a moral evaluation. Each particular situation has to be evaluated separately and this inclines some philosophers to argue that there are no general moral principles of any kind. Thus Jonathan Dancy thinks that because there can be inconsistency in moral judgments it is misleading to discuss them in relation to general principles. In his paper 'Ethical Relativism and Morally Relevant Properties'[4] he writes:

> The problem of consistency of principles really arises because of conflict in particular cases. Particularist epistemology tells us that moral knowledge comes from our knowledge of cases. One relevant thing we can observe in a case is that two properties are militating against each other there.[5]

Dancy argues that those who rely on moral principles have to explain the conflict of such principles in particular situations and he suggests that individuals do *not* rely on general principles when making a moral choice. Rather he thinks that in any given situation each person 'picks out' features judged to be morally relevant and that the conflict between two features of the situation is not best treated as a conflict between moral principles. He considers that it is simply not helpful to support moral judgments by appealing to general moral principles and so, in effect, he is saying that there are no such principles. Therefore he denies that there are *general* morally relevant properties of situations; that is he says that there are no general or universal principles to which we can appeal when we make a moral judgment or assessment of any particular case. He espouses the cause of ethical particularism, and in support of his views he compares moral evaluations with aesthetic descriptions –

descriptions which will carry overtones of aesthetic evaluation:

> In such a description, certain features will be mentioned as salient within the context of the building as a whole. There is no thought that such features will be *generally* salient; they matter here and that is enough. Someone offering the description is telling his audience how to see the building the right way.[6]

Similarly the salient features of a moral situation are pointed out so that:

> The man who provides reasons is not so much providing evidence for his ethical judgements as trying to show his audience how he sees the situation. He supposes that to see it his way is to join in with his judgement about what is right and wrong; so if you do come to see it his way you will agree with his ethical judgement, but by giving his reasons he is not *arguing* for that judgement, in the way which adherents of moral principles might suppose.[7]

An analogous account of explanations of non-moral actions, done to fulfil desires, is given by Stuart Hampshire:

> When it comes to giving an account of the reasons for an action, or course of conduct, one picks out a few salient desires and beliefs from the foreground of consciousness and, more specifically, those that distinguish this particular occasion and this particular person: . . . Even in the case of action following upon fully explicit deliberation, and of a contemporary account of the reasons for the decision, the reasons are a selection of the interesting items, and are recognised as being a selection.[8]

Now of course we can agree that reasons for actions, be the actions selfish or altruistic, will be in terms of certain salient features; backgrounds will be taken for granted by those who explain and by those who receive the explanation. It is also true that explanations of moral behaviour will carry an invitation to others to assess likewise. We know that it is possible that others may assess a situation differently and, where morality is concerned, we want people at least to understand how we see things. We may well try to get them to agree with us by appeals to emotion, trying to persuade by non-rational means. But we may prefer to use rational moral argument. Both persuasion and argument presuppose a common background of moral principles that transcend particular situations. It is these moral principles which, like the moral directives embodied in institutional facts, make ethical assessment possible. Just *because* they are taken for granted they are not explicitly stated.

An example of moral conflict is given by Jean-Paul Sartre: a young man living in France in 1941 must choose whether to join the Free French forces in England or stay at home in France with his mother. She will be alone without him for she is alienated from her husband (his father) who is collaborating with the Nazis. Her elder son, the young man's elder brother, has been killed fighting for the Nazis. The young man wishes to avenge the death of his brother, by joining the Free French army, but he knows that his mother depends on him and that if he went away she would be plunged into despair and might die. He has to evaluate what is the morally best thing to do bearing in mind that his departure will certainly cause despair whereas his contribution to the Free French cause would probably be negligible.

> He also realised that, concretely and in fact, every action he performed on his mother's behalf would be sure of an effect in the sense of aiding her to live, whereas anything he did in order to go and fight would be an ambiguous action which might vanish like water into sand and serve no purpose . . . he found himself confronted by two very different modes of action; the one concrete, immediate, but directed towards only one individual; and the other action addressed to an end infinitely greater, a national collectivity, but for that very reason ambiguous – and it might be frustrated on the way. At the same time, he was hesitating between two kinds of morality; on the one side the morality of sympathy of personal devotion and, on the other side, a morality of wider scope but of more debateable validity. He had to choose between these two.[9]

Sartre may have thought that the validity of the second kind of morality was debatable because the motive was partly vengeance and not purely a matter of duty. He argues that there is no 'right' solution to this conflict; different people will make different choices. In Dancy's terms, different people would pick out different features that they see as salient features; either choice can be the right moral choice in that it is the right course of action for the person who makes that choice. Nevertheless a choice will only be a morally rational choice if it can be shown to be supported by one of the basic moral principles. Disagreement about choice will be a disagreement about priorities, and to say that two people make a different choice and yet both have acted morally and rightly is not necessarily contradictory.[10] It need not be contradictory because the motives and character of the chooser affect the morality and rationality of the choice.

Thus the fact that different people (or even the same person at different times) can make different but equally acceptable rational moral judgments is an important feature of such judgments. Sartre says that if values are uncertain nothing remains but to trust our instincts, but I suggest that we can trust our instincts only because we have our two basic principles firmly established.

Dancy prefers to talk about how people *see* a moral situation, that is he prefers to talk about moral descriptions that imply a moral judgment, rather than to talk directly about such judgments. This is because he wants to avoid invoking moral principles. Now if ethical assessments were just a matter of each person picking out what she considered to be salient moral features, clearly they would be subjective. But, in addition, if this were all there were to these assessments, they could not be moral judgments; for, as indicated above, salient moral features can only be picked out as *moral* features if some moral principles are presupposed. However, Dancy's account of moral evaluation does help us to understand how two opposing judgments, leading to the decisions to take different courses of action, are not contradictory. Different people are likely to pick out different salient features; they see the situation in different ways even though both relate their particular salient features to the same fundamental moral principles. We can compare this to two different aesthetic judgments as Dancy does, and even to two different empirical judgments made from physically different positions, thus giving, literally, different points of view.

The character of each judge gives her a moral point of view but, unlike a physical position, what decision the judge takes, after judgment, and what actions follow that decision, will themselves affect the character of the judge. We *make* and develop our characters largely by judging and acting on our decisions as moral agents. If we choose to act wrongly our characters will deteriorate. If we act rightly we shall strengthen our moral awareness. This is close to Sartre's existentialist view that we are what we are by what we *choose* to do. It is also related to Aristotle's account of responsibility: we make ourselves good or bad, and cannot appeal to weakness of will or our own nature to absolve ourselves of that responsibility:

> 'Well, probably he is the sort of person that doesn't take care.'
> But people get into this condition through their own fault, by
> the slackness of their lives; i.e. they make themselves unjust or
> licentious by behaving dishonestly or spending their time in
> drinking and other forms of dissipation; for in every sphere of
> conduct people develop qualities corresponding to the activities
> that they pursue. This is evident from the example of people
> training for any competition or undertaking: they spend all their
> lives in exercising. So to be unaware that in every department of
> conduct moral states are the result of corresponding activities is
> the mark of a thoroughly unperceptive person.[11]

And:

> Therefore virtue lies in our power, and similarly so does vice;
> because where it is in our power to act, it is also in our power not
> to act, and where we can refuse we can also comply. . . . And if
> it is in our power to do right and wrong, and similarly not to do
> them: and if, . . . doing right or wrong is the essence of being
> good or bad, it follows that it is in our power to be decent or
> worthless.[12]

Sartre stresses that each person can and must make a moral law to guide her actions, and thereby makes her own character:

> Certainly we cannot say that this man, in choosing to remain
> with his mother – that is, in taking sentiment, personal devotion
> and concrete charity as his moral foundations – would be
> making an irresponsible choice, nor could we do so if he
> preferred the sacrifice of going away to England. Man makes
> himself; he is not found ready-made; he cannot but choose a
> morality, such is the pressure of circumstances upon him.[13]

He goes so far as to say that we invent values, and that these invented values are the values by which we live:

> . . . to say that we invent values means neither more nor less
> than this; that there is no sense in life *a priori*. Life is nothing

112

until it is lived; but it is yours to make sense of, and the value of it is nothing else but the sense you choose.[14]

Here it is maintained that the basic moral principles must guide any person's moral choice of values but the existentialist position does help us to understand how it is that there can be more than one rational moral choice in any situation. To be aware of this is to enhance our own moral appreciation of particular situations and of moral judgments in general.

X

SECONDARY PRINCIPLES AND SOCIAL VALUES

We have seen that a distinctive feature of moral judgments is that the particular circumstances of each situation can profoundly affect moral assessment so that even though we have the basic principles as general guides, it is rare to arrive at a judgment that can be applicable without qualification to a variety of situations. For the basic principles are not specific and we do not normally appeal to them directly when making moral evaluations and moral judgments. Their chief use is to support derived or secondary principles. As we shall see, secondary principles are still general principles, and they can be taken as the 'working principles' of a society. They support the currently accepted moral values of the society – or at least are *believed* to support those values by most members of it. I shall call the moral values of a given society its *social values*. 'Social values' is a less misleading term than 'moral values' since the latter can imply that they transcend social custom (which they do not) and that they are sacrosanct (which they are not).

Observation of alien societies, and records of laws and customs in the same society at different times, plainly show that social values are diverse and even that they can conflict. In addition we know from direct experience that current social values in our own society are and have been questioned and that changes (some relatively slow, some quite quick) occur. We may personally be in doubt as to the validity of some of the social values that we were brought up to accept. Indeed one reason why social values, and their supporting secondary principles, are thought to be more fundamental than they really are, and hence why certain values are erroneously thought to be fundamental, is that moral teaching in childhood

114

has a very great influence on us all.

As we grow up and develop as moral beings our innate capacity for moral awareness is elicited by observation of behaviour which we and others assess in relation to moral precepts. As was stated in chapter VI (page 80) we do not learn the fundamental principles and then derive the secondary principles from them; it is the other way round. In fact we start at a less basic level than the secondary principles for we first become aware of specific obligations and duties and specific acts of benevolence and we are taught relatively specific moral precepts. Later we may come to understand that duties can be regarded as arising from the moral need to act in accordance with the supporting secondary principles.

Our developing moral sense is also helped and reinforced by the language that we and those around us use. As we saw in chapter VII, language makes us aware of moral obligations as institutional facts – what *is*, contains an implied *ought*. Many secondary principles derived from obligation and some of those connected with benevolence can be formulated as institutional facts. For example, it is understood that to make a promise is to incur a moral obligation to fulfil that promise and, in our society at least, it is, again as we saw in chapter VII, an institutional fact that promising carries an *obligation* (moral and in some cases legal). Likewise it is an institutional fact that to show mercy is to refrain from vengeance and this institutional fact constitutes a moral act of benevolence. Secondary principles are also explicitly taught us – we hear them as moral commandments and we also hear them praised.

There are a variety of reasons for there being different secondary principles and social values in different societies, and indeed within societies:[1] differences in geographical situation and climate, differences in background empirical knowledge, different religious beliefs and different conventions and customs. But in the end a decision to reject or to accept a secondary principle must be based on appeal to a primary principle; it is only primary principles that need no justification. Unfortunately much moral discussion within a society and also between societies cannot be understood as discussion as to how the primary principles (that are common to all and accepted by all) relate to the moral issues being considered. This is partly a result of prejudice and also a reluctance to accept that even the most treasured secondary principles *are* secondary and so need to be justified. Our human tendency to generalise, and to warm to generalisations, tempts us all to devise general rules (that we like to think are universally applicable), from observation of relatively few (and generally local) situations. We disregard the fact that these rules are possibly inapplicable, without much modification, to other situations. In addition we face the empirical complexity of moral problems: relevant facts can rarely be established and consequences cannot be reliably predicted.

As stated above, secondary principles, even if established and well-known within a given society, will not necessarily be universally commended and may well be questioned even within the society concerned. For example, in Britain in the late twentieth century the general belief is that it is right that an accused person should have a public trial and that, for any serious offence attracting a prison sentence, the verdict should be found by a jury; but there are some who argue that trial by jury is not necessary in *all* criminal cases. In some other countries it is generally acceptable that there should be no jury and, indeed, no public trial. Again, the majority of people in Britain today think that it is right that children should be educated and that their parents should be required to see that they attend school, but a few think that schools are unnecessary and that there should be no coercion. Yet again most people in Britain now think that if a human foetus is known to be malformed, or even if there is a high probability that it will be malformed, then clinical abortion is morally (and legally) permissible; but some people disagree, and disagree strongly. Any debate on such issues must be based on knowledge of the empirical facts, including medical facts, and also on appeal to the fundamental moral principles.

These examples also serve to illustrate the hypothetical character of secondary principles: the great majority of British people think that an accused person *ought* to have an open trial by jury but, in certain cases where national security would be at risk, they allow that a trial may be *in camera* for the state's obligations to citizens in general is here considered to outweigh the duties to one individual or group. Likewise we think that children *ought* to go to school but we allow that parents who can show that they can educate their children at home may keep them from school. The right of a mother to bear a malformed baby is not, of course, in question for legislation on abortion is not concerned with enforcing the destruction of a foetus but with permitting it (in defined circumstances) *if* the mother so wishes.

As we saw in chapter VII, parental care of infant children is a secondary principle derived from the primary principle of keeping trust; state care can also be derived from this principle – in a sense we are all vicarious parents of the children in our society. What is held to constitute care varies in different societies and has changed in our own society within the past century to a very marked extent. Care of children has always had a high social value of course but the particular obligations, and the particular acts and kind of behaviour expected of the state and of parents, have changed and will continue to change. In addition, as with all moral situations, the empirical circumstances of each case have a profound effect on any evaluation. This is why when we make moral judgments as to how good a parent a particular person is, or what society tolerates in the treatment of a given child or group of children, we have to be careful to take account of the facts of the background knowledge and beliefs as well as the facts of the particular situation.

The effect of empirical circumstances on secondary moral principles is shown by the changed moral attitudes to normal pregnancy care and to abortion. We now know that the healthy development and growth of a foetus is partly a matter of genetic make-up and that it is also closely related to the health of the mother. It is now considered a moral duty for doctors to advise mothers to eat sensibly, to avoid smoking and drinking and to try to avoid contracting certain diseases such as *rubella*. In addition the state is held to have a moral duty to publicise this advice. The mother is not legally required to follow it but there is not negligible moral pressure to do so. This is largely a result of increased knowledge of foetal development and maternal health.

However we do not rule out the possibility that a mother has an absolute right (moral and legal) to terminate her pregnancy, at least in the early stages, even if the potential child would almost certainly be healthy. Thus a secondary moral principle of duty of care appears to conflict with a secondary moral principle of autonomy. The moral assessment of abortion, and our view of the foetus, has changed. Although a healthy foetus is undeniably a future or a potential person, many people now think that it does not have the status of an actual person, and, in particular that it is not owed the same moral concern. (This is not to say that it is of no moral concern, as we shall see later.) There are empirical reasons for this change. Firstly, the increase in medical knowledge has shown us that the foetus develops from a blob of protoplasm that cannot in itself be sentient; in addition medical advances make abortions safe.[2] Secondly, the decline in religious faith has led to fundamental changes in our attitude to human life – today many doubt that each human being has an immortal soul and there is even less support for the view that this soul is part of the individual from the moment of conception or at the quickening. Thirdly, there has been, as a result of individual and social pressures, a change in attitude to the status of women – it is not common nowadays to regard women as *just* mothers or potential mothers. Fourthly, because the background has changed, different views are now taken as to the moral implications for society in legalising abortion.

I do not think it is possible to know which of these changes has been most important in bringing about the present attitude(s) to abortion. It is likely that those who do not dismiss abortion as immoral are most influenced by the developments in physiology but this must be because they take religious faith to be irrelevant and because they do not question that women should have as much autonomy as men. The view that physiological factors are paramount explains why the morality of abortion is related to the age of the foetus and the circumstances of the mother. Most people think that a foetus can become an object of moral concern before it acquires the status of a person. Thus Peter Singer has argued that after birth the neonate does not have the same right to moral concern as an adult,[3] but even when he argued that there would be no immorality *per se* in killing a month-old baby he condemned abortion methods, such as suction, that were likely to cause pain to the foetus.

Singer has since modified his views on neonates and is now in agreement with Michael Lockwood; Lockwood proposes that an embryo should become a matter of moral concern when its *life*, as opposed to its existence, begins. By 'life' he means 'sentience' because he argues that sentience is the characteristic of the *biographical life* of any individual. It is an empirical fact that sentience is possible with the appearance of neural structures, the beginning of the embryo brain, and Lockwood suggests that (biographical) life starts with brain life and ends with brain death.[4] Hence he concludes that abortion on demand is morally permissible up to the appearances of neural structures (about ten weeks) but that after that the foetus becomes an object of moral concern in its own right and its future, as well as its mother's, needs to be considered. Readers of this book will have varying views as to the morality of abortion. Here I am not concerned with the debate itself; I have referred to it as an illustration of empirical facts profoundly affecting moral issues related to secondary principles.

In our society we also acknowledge a social and family duty of care to the mentally defective and the mentally ill; this has not always been the case. Perfunctory as the exercise of this duty can be at the present time, it is acknowledged as a duty and the contrast with the code of obligation of some two or three centuries ago is marked. In times past it was a duty to care for those who were physically ill but mental illness was regarded with suspicion or with amusement. The ill-educated thought that mental illness might be a punishment inflicted by God; others took mad and eccentric behaviour as a source of fun and were unaware of and therefore indifferent to the sufferings of neurotics and psychotics. Our present attitude to the insane and the mentally defective is not a consequence of our being more moral and having a stricter view of our obligations to those in difficulty, but to a different understanding of mental illness and of mental abnormalities. This is a result of advances in medical knowledge. We now see the behaviour of the sufferers as symptoms, i.e. as signs of illness analogous to physical illness, and therefore morally demanding sympathy and care.

There are other secondary moral principles that have developed as moral principles: today we regard public drunkenness as being much more immoral than it was held to be in the nineteenth century – especially the drunkenness of the relatively well-to-do.[5] This is largely because those who drink in public may well be driving cars and there are great risks, to the individual and to others, associated with drunken driving. To drink and to drive constitutes a serious breach of trust in that we become unacceptably dangerous to others and if we are dangerous we break our duty of care to others. So what was once thought to be a regrettable but relatively trivial debauchery, occasionally leading to tragedy, is now thought to be criminally irresponsible. As we saw in chapter VIII, our attitude to the treatment of animals is also gradually changing, so our moral principles respecting animals are changed. There is increasing support for movements aimed at enforcing and imposing laws restricting the use of animals in experiments, whether for advancing

119

the study of psychology, testing the efficacy and safety of drugs or investigating the side effects of cosmetics.

Another area of behaviour that is becoming subject to moral criticism is the disposal of waste, whether it be paper and bottles left on picnic sites or industrial waste and nuclear waste. We are beginning to accept that we have a *moral*[6] obligation to refrain from spoiling the countryside and from polluting the air and water. Major chemical and nuclear pollution is so dangerous that it would have been censured at earlier times if it had occurred but the minor pollution of leisure litter is regarded as much more immoral than it would have been a hundred years ago. With a larger population taking holidays and visiting beauty spots we have come to see that we have a moral obligation to control litter.

Another change that has occurred in recent decades is in our attitude to honesty and our interpretation of the secondary principle that it is right to act honestly. Our code of behaviour still excludes direct theft such as shoplifting, bank robbery and burglary but today there is a less disapproving attitude to various forms of fraud and pretty theft than obtained in, say, the nineteenth century. Many people who regard themselves as honest use stationery and allied materials provided at their place of work for their private correspondence. Indeed so common has this become that it is very often tacitly accepted by the employer. Thus what started as petty theft becomes condoned, or at least ignored. Then it has, of course, ceased to be a betrayal of trust. Many people do not think that evasion of paying income tax is a form of fraud and is as immoral as fraud. Indeed tax collectors are seriously worried at the change in moral attitudes to taxation because they are well aware that it is the conscience of each person that is the primary force in keeping her law-abiding. It is difficult enough to detect the few who are dishonest, but it would be impossible to track down widespread dishonesty. Therefore, as the particular form of dishonesty shown in tax evasion disturbs the conscience of individuals less and less, it becomes more and more difficult to catch evaders. This encourages yet more evasion: partly because it becomes clear that there is less risk of legal penalty, and partly because people who have been honest resent the unfairness – if rogues can get away with it why should honest people have to pay? This kind of reasoning itself shows that tax evasion is not thought of as ordinary fraud for if we hear that a person has beggared others by swindling them of their savings and has not been brought to justice we are unlikely to be tempted to behave in the same way in the hope that we too shall get away with it.

Our change in attitude to petty theft and tax evasion can be regarded as a change in our conception of honesty or as a modification of the secondary principle that it is right to be honest. In point of fact we want to act in accordance with the secondary principle of honesty since it is so closely related to the fundamental principle of keeping trust. So we arrange to avoid admitting that certain kinds of dishonest behaviour are dishonest by re-evaluating such behaviour. We may say that petty theft from an employer is too trivial to be regarded as a serious breaking of trust and is therefore not dishonest. We may say that tax evasion is a way of avoiding an unjust sequestration of *our* money; here the dishonest behaviour is justified by appeal to what are taken to be more important and therefore overriding secondary principles. By re-evaluating (and, since fact and value are so closely related, by redescribing) we modify the concept of honesty and defend our own wish to remain honest.

Sometimes a change in moral attitudes and social codes leads not to a modification of a moral concept but to the relegation of a secondary principle. A principle that is relegated ceases to act as a guide to behaviour and the moral prescription that we ought to act in accordance with the principle disappears. For example, sexual fidelity was a highly rated moral quality, particularly as an attribute of women; it was seen as an important form of keeping trust.[7] As we read in the discussion of the value overtones of 'chaste' in chapter III, and of the institution of marriage in chapter VII, it was expected that women, and *a fortiori* wives, would be sexually faithful. Doubtless this arose from a desire to be certain of the paternity of children. The reason for a different attitude today, on the part of a significant number of members of our society, is partly due to the emergence of new attitudes to women, and the life they do or might lead, and partly a result of increased knowledge of contraceptive methods. The change in attitude to sexual fidelity is not a change in the attitude to the principle of keeping trust; it is simply that those who accept the new moral attitude do not regard sexual fidelity as part of the essence of keeping trust.

If we compare codes of much earlier times with our own the changes are much greater. We noted various examples of changing codes in chapter VII; each change represents a modified secondary principle. In particular there was, in times past, a strict duty of host to guest. Today if we learned that a person who was staying in our house as a guest was wanted by the police we should not necessarily regurd it as our duty to help that friend. We might warn her, that would depend on the circumstances, but protection would not be seen as the overriding obligation that it would have been in medieval times. Our codes of behaviour relating to the human embryo, care of the mentally ill, taking of property, paying tax, treatment of animals, etc. have all been modified. There are changes in the empirical facts that have led to a change in our *moral* attitudes. Some practices are condemned more strongly, some less strongly; there have been changes in concepts and also changes in the moral force of secondary principles. It is at the secondary level that moral attitudes vary so much; the social values that they support are the current values of society. Secondary principles are bound up with the customs and conventions of society, and their *relationship* to the primary principles can and will change as circumstances change and as empirical knowledge changes. But the *primary* principles remain unchanged.

The examples considered have been comparisons of our current moral attitudes with those of former times but there are analogous differences of secondary principles among contemporaries in different places. For example, in some parts of the Middle East it is regarded as a just punishment for theft to cut off the hand of the thief; in Spain and Mexico bull-fighting is thought to be an enjoyable entertainment and not immoral cruelty: it is said that in some African countries slavery is still acceptable. We may regard some or all of these practices as immoral and doubtless some of our practices, our treatment of elderly relatives and our tolerations of abortion for example, would be regarded as immoral in other countries.

In his article 'Ethics, Mathematics and Relativism'[8] Jonathan Lear compares ethical disputes with mathematical disputes. He suggests that we cannot give a coherent account of a group that believed that '7 + 5 = 13'[9] for this belief could not be accommodated with other arithmetical and non-arithmetical beliefs so as to give an understandable picture of the behaviour of the group. He says that mathematics is considered to be objective because, despite the inapplicability of Euclidean geometry, mathematics does mirror the world as we understand it:[10]

> Thus a mathematical statement like '7 + 5 = 12' is true in virtue
> of its applicability to the world: and we can understand how it is
> applicable because we can see that mathematics preserves
> structural features that are to be found in the physical world.[11]

But though we cannot give a coherent account of a group that did
not accept our simple arithmetic, the case is different when we
consider possible differences in approach to, say, the mathematical
notion of infinity, as suggested by Cantor in his development of
transfinite arithmetic.[12] Lear considers the case of a tribe that did
not accept transfinite arithmetic and the way that their chief might
justify the non-acceptance:

> 'Imagine', the chief begins, 'that you and I have been in
> existence throughout the previous history of the world. Our
> physical and mental characteristics change fairly continuously
> and though our memories are much stronger than ordinary
> human memories they have the same basic nature: . . .
> Although we have been in existence during the entire previous
> history of the world, we are not immortal. In fact God has
> scheduled it so that I must die today and you have been granted
> another eighty years to live.
>
> 'I am inclined to think,' the chief continues, 'that God has
> granted you eighty *more* years to live than me. And I'm sure if
> we asked any of your people who had not studied your theory of
> transfinite arithmetic, this would be their untutored response.
> However, according to your theory. . . . If . . . the previous
> history of the world extends endlessly into the past, then . . .
> you will not live any more days than me.'[13]

Now we can certainly gives a coherent account of a group's way of
life even if the group does not accept transfinite arithmetic. This is
quite a different matter from trying to make sense of the beliefs and
way of life of a tribe that held that '7 + 5 = 13'. Simple arithmetic
and simple arithmetical sums are and must be basically the same
everywhere if we are to make sense of the way people think. The
principles of simple arithmetic correspond to fundamental moral
principles and we can only make sense of the beliefs and behaviour
of human societies that accept both the principles of simple arithmetic and the two fundamental moral principles. Both kinds of

principle are universal in that they mirror the world and human behaviour as we perceive and understand them. The theorems of transfinite arithmetic correspond to secondary moral principles; both are culture-dependent. We still might be able to give grounds for preferring transfinite arithmetic and for preferring some secondary principles in all cultures. We might be able to show that transfinite arithmetic gave more helpful methods for dealing with certain types of mathematical problem and we might justify certain secondary moral principles objectively by showing that they were closely related to one or both primary principles.

Lear shows how what appears to be a conflict of secondary moral principles may not be a conflict of *moral* principles at all. He considers two societies with different ways of treating their dead: in one the dead are burned, in the other they are eaten. Each group thinks that the custom of the other is morally obnoxious but there is no serious moral issue here; the conflicts are not analogous to those discussed in chapter IX. The moral issue is not serious because the dead themselves have no feelings.[14] Each custom acceptable to the local community can be tolerated by others and this does not entail any *ethical* relativism. The toleration is analogous to toleration of different styles of dress, different ways of greeting, different sexual conventions and different marriage rituals. We may think that the practice of eating the dead is repugnant but it is not *morally* repugnant.

Ethical relativism involves the toleration of behaviour that is *morally* repugnant on the grounds that an alien society must be judged by its social values, not those of the observer. The distaste arises not as a result of the bizarre or unaesthetic nature of the practices but because we judge that they are based on invalid (secondary) principles – either not related to a primary principle or based on an erroneous assessment of the facts. For example, certain marriage customs do not just involve strange but ethically neutral behaviour, they require wives to be treated as total subordinates. In some countries widows are not allowed to remarry, even if still very young. The people of these countries believe that their custom can be morally justified; we would dispute this because we have different secondary moral principles which incline us to a different code of behaviour. The situation is analogous to the chief who did not accept transfinite arithmetic and disagreed with our own mathematician who did accept it. Just as there was scope for mathematical debate in that case, so there is scope for ethical debate in these cases. But until such time as this can be arranged we are prepared to tolerate situations elsewhere that we would not tolerate in our own society.

Lastly there will be customs that we believe flout not only some of our secondary moral principles but also one or both of the two primary principles; for example the practice of burning widows with their husband's corpse. When we learn of such customs we have active moral concern; we may believe that we are justified in using force to make people abandon the custom. Alternatively we shall want to engage in moral debate because we would be convinced that we could show how the custom violates fundamental ethical principles that we know that all human beings respect. We think that those who practice widow-burning, slavery, torture and apartheid must be brought to change their ways.

An ethical debate is conducted in order to get agreement on a moral matter. We believe that we are right and we want to get our opponents to change their moral attitudes and to make the same moral judgments that we make. It can be analogous to a mathematical debate, on the merits of transfinite arithmetic at secondary level, or on the *necessity*[15] to add in a certain way at the primary level. It is also analogous to a dispute as to the merits of two scientific theories, say Ptolemy's and Copernicus's, at the secondary level; or to a dispute about whether there are physical objects at the primary level. In all three types of dispute, ethical, mathematical and empirical, we seek to change opinions and beliefs, and we wish to change them by appeals to reason not by appeal to subjective feelings. In mathematical debates we seek to show that a theory will give a more satisfying and more elegant system than its rival; at the basic level we seek to show that a bizarre simple arithmetic will undermine the entire mathematical system. In scientific debate we seek to show that facts as interpreted by one theory will give a more satisfying account of events perceived and that this theory will be a basis for more accurate predictions than its rival; at the basic level we seek to show that refusal to structure sensory evidence will make it impossible to have any empirical knowledge. In ethical debate we seek to show that *our* secondary moral principles make for realisation of the values that are embodied in the primary principles; at the basic level we seek to show that certain types of behaviour are incompatible with a human moral society.

XI

MORALITY AND THE LAW

En passant, there has already been reference to the interaction of the law and morality in chapters VI and X. Secondary moral principles and social values clearly affect the decisions to make laws and the content, interpretation and enforcement of these; they also give reason to respect the law. This is not to say that there is no distinction between the law and moral principles. Utilitarian philosophers such as Jeremy Bentham (1748–1831) and John Austin (1790–1859) stressed this distinction, a distinction which Professor Hart gives as 'law as it is from law as it ought to be'.[1] Austin was clear that moral principles, enjoined by God and supported by the principle of utility, did (or should) guide conduct. For him it was the only guide, for he did not believe that human beings had any other means of making moral judgments.

> And first, if utility be our only index to the tact commands of the Deity, it is idle to object to its imperfections. We must even make the most of it.
>
> If we were endowed with a *moral sense*, or with a *common sense*, or with a *practical reason*, we scarcely should construe his commands by the principle of general utility. . . .
>
> But, if we are not gifted with that peculiar organ, we must take to the principle of utility, let it be never so defective. We must gather our duties, as we can, from the tendencies of human actions; or remain, at our own peril, in ignorance of our duties. We must pick our scabrous way with the help of a glimmering light, or wander in profound darkness.[2]

Hart quotes from the same work to show that Austin separated moral from legal conduct, albeit a law not compatible with moral principles (for Austin this meant the principle of utility) was a bad law:

> The existence of law is one thing; its merit or demerit is another. Whether it be or be not is one enquiry; whether it be or be not conformable to an assumed standard, is a different enquiry. A law, which actually exists, is a law, though we happen to dislike it, or though it vary from text to text, by which we regulate our approbation and disapprobation.[3]

And Hart himself says:

> What both Bentham and Austin were anxious to assert were the following two simple things: first, in the absence of an expressed constitutional or legal provision, it could not follow from the mere fact that a rule violated standards of morality that it was not a rule of law; and, conversely, it could not follow from the mere fact that a rule was morally desirable that it was a rule of law.[4]

In this chapter we shall consider the reasons for there being laws at all, and views taken about the relationship between the law and moral principles.

Human beings are social creatures who are morally aware, yet they also naturally egotistical. Hence though all of us acknowledge that there must be agreed codes of conduct for the smooth running of society and for personal fulfilment, most of us also agree that there must a system of law to clarify the code and there must also be a means of enforcing the code. Since this is in fact the case in our own society (and in others) it becomes a matter of prudence to obey the law – whether it is also a matter of morality we will now investigate.

There are anarchists who think that government and a system of formal laws enforced by threat of punishment are not necessary; but even they do not think that it is possible to live with our fellows without any basis of accepted codes of behaviour. They differ from most of us in thinking that a legal system and policing are not required. Thus a discussion of laws, considered as codes for guiding behaviour, does not necessarily presuppose the Law, along with its enforcement; it is possible to discuss the ethics of laws without considering their implementation. Nevertheless, though much of what we shall consider in this chapter would apply to an anarchic society, we shall reserve the terms 'law' and 'the Law' for formal rules that are enforced by the state by means of penalties for transgression.

Not all laws are made to support moral principles: some are rules for cooperative behaviour, rules that in themselves have no moral force whatsoever: they are explicit rules of convenience. It is clear that there is no moral principle determining on which side of the road we should drive our cars, or on what day we should introduce summer time, or whether we should adopt a decimalised currency. But once a rule has been decided then it does become a matter of morality (as well as prudence) to conform. Flouting of such rules will lead to personal inconvenience as well as attracting punishment, but morality is involved because others will be inconvenienced, and perhaps endangered, if the rules are ignored or broken. Therefore, in general, those who break laws that are rules of convenience, non-moral in themselves, will incur social disapproval – the disapproval accorded to members of the group who take no care to co-operate. This disapproval can be just as strong as the disapproval of those who break laws that are directly related to moral principles.

So, whether a given law is a mere rule of convenience, which we obey because it is necessary to co-operate with others, or whether it reflects and supports a moral principle, we are under a *prima facie* moral obligation to conform. Co-operation with others is to fulfil their reasonable expectations and, as we saw in chapter VII, this is part of the moral duty of members of a society, a duty derived from the primary moral principle of keeping trust. The government of the state employs officers to maintain laws and to detect offenders but it is not only detection and punishment which keeps us, in the main, law-abiding. As was noted in chapter X, the great majority of us are brought up to respect the moral codes of our society and the laws that, by and large, support them, and we conform to the law most of the time without constant supervision or threat of punishment. Most of us feel guilty if we break laws that embody moral principles because our self-respect demands that in all matters that we regard as important we behave morally.[5] In general we do not have the same regard for laws that are rules of convenience but we are concerned to co-operate most of the time because we desire the esteem and respect of others.[6] This desire also plays an important part in helping to keep most of us conforming to the moral codes and respecting the social values of our fellows and so, in general, abiding by the law.

There are differences of opinion about the role of accepted social values, the general attitude to behaviour, in the making and the enforcement of laws. Thus in his criticism of the Wolfenden Report on Homosexual Offences and Prostitution Lord Devlin writes:

> It is clear that the criminal law as we know it is based upon moral principle. In a number of crimes its function is simply to enforce a moral principle and nothing else. The law, both criminal and civil, claims to be able to speak about morality and immorality generally. Where does it get its authority to do this and how does it settle the moral principles which it enforces? Undoubtedly, as a matter of history, it derived both from Christian teaching. But I think the strict logician is right when he says that the law can no longer rely on doctrines in which citizens are entitled to disbelieve. It is necessary therefore to look for some other source.[7]

He recognises that laws against treason are designed to protect society, for an established government is necessary for the existence of any society.

> But an established morality is as necessary as good government to the welfare of society. Societies disintegrate from within more frequently than they are broken up be external pressures. There is disintegration when no common morality is observed and history shows that the loosening of moral bonds is often the first stage of disintegration, so that society is justified in taking the same steps to preserve its moral code as it does to preserve its government and other essential institutions.[8]

And *what* is that moral code? Devlin suggests:

> English law has evolved and regularly uses a standard which does not depend on the counting of heads. It is that of the reasonable man. He is not to be confused with the rational man. He is not to be expected to reason about anything and his judgment may be largely a matter of feeling. It is the viewpoint of the man in the street – or to use an archaism familiar to all lawyers – the man in the Clapham omnibus. He might also be

called the right-minded man. For my purpose I should like to
call him the man in the jury box, for the moral judgement of
society must be something about which any twelve men or
women drawn at random might, after discussion, be expected to
be unanimous.[9]

He admits[10] that the limits of tolerance shift, but laws, especially
those based on morals, must be slow to move for public opinion may
be only temporarily changed.

This view is explicitly opposed by Professor Hart. He agrees that
there must be an agreed consensus of moral opinion:

> But it does not follow that everything to which the moral vetoes
> of accepted morality attach is of equal importance to
> society. . . . Surely even in the face of the moral feeling that is
> up to concert pitch – the trio of intolerance, indignation and
> disgust – we must pause to think.[11]

Hart objects to Devlin's comparison of offences such as treason
with personal (in particular, sexual) immorality, but his principal
reason for opposing Devlin's view is that Devlin appears to Hart to
be appealing to moral emotions rather than to moral reasons. Hart
says:

> When Sir Patrick's lecture was first delivered *The Times* greeted
> it with these words: 'There is a moving and welcome humility in
> the conception that society should not be asked to give its reason
> for refusing to tolerate what in its heart it feels intolerable.' This
> drew from a correspondent in Cambridge the retort: 'I am afraid
> that we are less humble than we used to be. We once burnt old
> women because, without giving our reasons, we felt in our
> hearts that witchcraft was intolerable.'[12]

Professor Hart has scored an easy point but there is some confusion
here. Witchcraft would be thought intolerable if there were such a
thing. The readers of this book, along with the man on the Clapham
omnibus, do not believe that there is (or was) any genuine evidence
for the existence of witches or witchcraft in the medieval sense.[13]
This is taken as a matter of fact and neither moral attitudes nor
emotions are involved. However the example does reveal a change
in moral attitudes and social values because, unlike the people of
the sixteenth century, our society would not tolerate burning for

any offence. To some extent this change can be said to be the result of moral reason for such punishment is incompatible with the primary moral principle of benevolence. But there is a powerful emotional element also, for it is the contemporary emotional revulsion against burning which makes it unnecessary to *argue* that no person should be burned.

Moral reason and moral emotion cannot be separated in moral judgment; as we saw in chapter V our moral sense may be compared with our aesthetic sense. When we consider the relation between the law and moral attitudes we have a further complication based on the fact that because laws alter our behaviour they can bring about an alteration in moral attitudes and social values. It is too simplistic to imply that laws support morals, for the law and moral attitudes are *inter*dependent. Lord Devlin wrote in 1965 and censure of homosexuality, which seemed perhaps conservative but reasonable then, is out of place now. During the course of twenty years the laws allowing homosexuals to associate more freely and overtly have led to greater public tolerance and understanding; many, like Devlin (and indeed perhaps Devlin himself) who opposed relaxation of the original restraining laws would not now support reimposition of the restraints. Likewise it is hoped that laws forbidding incitement to racial hatred will also help to bring about a change in attitude such that the law itself will become virtually redundant.

There are many examples of laws affecting attitudes and social values: since women have been entitled to vote, general attitudes to what ought (morally) to be the proper concern of women have changed; today no one questions the legal right of women to vote and to hold public office. Again the laws requiring employers to give their employees adequate notice for termination of employment, to pay redundancy money and to inform employees of conditions of service have made employers more aware of their responsibilities in a moral as well as a legal sense. Similarly laws stipulating a proper concern for safety at work, binding on employees and employers, have changed attitudes to the need for safety measures.

In another essay[14] Hart considers the view expressed by Devlin (see quote 8) and by Durkheim that the law needs to support established morality because otherwise social cohesion would be lost and therefore society itself would be undermined – this is why. Devlin thought himself justified in comparing personal immorality with treason. Hart points out that this will be tautologously true if we *define* a society by its current social values but, short of this, there is no evidence to support the view. It is clear that societies can cohere as social values change; British society did not disintegrate with changing attitudes to punishment. Devlin and Durkheim do acknowledge that some changes in morality are non-malignant and are not socially disruptive and, as we have seen (note 10) Devlin allows for 'tolerance shift'. Hart points out that there should be criteria for distinguishing such 'natural and non-malignant' changes from those that might be disruptive. He implies that none are offered. Of course Hart is right; social values are not fixed and major changes, often occurring quickly, do not lead to the disintegration of society. However, our discussion does show a very profound interdependence of law and values. It also shows that human beings depend on emotions as well as reason and, since the law deals with human beings, it is right that the part played by emotions be recognised.

The powerful influence of others' moral attitudes is shown by the fact that laws tend to be broken rather readily if detection of the transgression does not bring public disapproval. We must of course bear in mind that if there is no public disapproval the conscience of the individual may also not censure, so that there will be little or no internal sanction *as well as* no risk of incurring great public censure and shame. We have seen (chapter X) that tax collectors are worried by the public tolerance of tax evasion; other examples of laws that are frequently disregarded are those forbidding parking in certain areas and at certain times, those imposing speed limits in towns and on motorways, those concerned with Sunday shopping and those ordering payment of maintenance allowances. The circumstances in which they are broken are circumstances in which they are not regarded as being morally significant or, as in the last example (and possibly in the case of some tax evaders), the individual believes them to be morally reprehensible. The lack of moral significance is shown by the fact that people who break these laws are not socially ostracised in the way that a rapist or a swindler or a burglar would be.

By contrast there are certain actions that we would condemn as immoral even though they are not illegal: deliberate unkindness, meanness[15] – people who are known to behave in such ways may well be ostracised. As we saw in chapter VI, laws are designed to

132

enforce the keeping of obligations rather than to enforce benevolence, but we do think that a certain minimum of benevolence ought (morally) to be shown. Though no one is morally censured for failing to show benevolence in any one instance, a total lack of benevolence will attract disapproval – moral disapproval. It is not contradictory to say that a certain person is immoral even though she has never broken the law.

In his book *Guide to the Philosophy of Morals and Politics*,[16] C.E.M. Joad suggests that there is a concept of social righteousness which lies between law and personal morality. It represents what are accepted codes of behaviour based on secondary moral principles, and it may be the code of a sub-group rather than a code of the whole society. Each individual's personal moral code is linked to and is (generally) supported by the code of her sub-group,[17] and the code of the sub-group is linked to but (generally) differs in some respects from the code of the society as a whole. Though moral conflict[18] between an individual and the law is always possible, the more serious conflicts arise between sub-groups and the law, i.e. where the sub-group's notion of social righteousness is opposed to some current law, or set of laws, and perhaps also to some aspect of the generally accepted moral code, or of the social values. The sub-group may be in a minority, and if the strength of their moral objection is great they will seek public attention and sympathy by protesting and perhaps also by campaigning for a change in the law and for a change in moral attitudes. They will appeal for support, primarily on moral grounds.

People who campaign for changes in the law are aware that their social values are, in relevant respects, not those that are respected by the majority of their fellows. Campaigners try to alter social values, possibly by emotional appeal (non-rational persuasion), but also through moral argument. They may seek to challenge the generally accepted secondary principles either by showing that they are not related to the universally accepted fundamental principles or by showing that they do not guide behaviour in the way that the majority assume that they do. The latter is partly an empirical argument, and there may be further empirical argument based on appeal to evidence showing that the assumed consequences of the current moral code and law do not in fact follow.

For example, the abolition of the law imposing a death penalty for murder was brought about by a campaign to change social values

133

and moral attitudes, in particular the values and attitudes of people such as Members of Parliament, who are directly responsible for making laws, and others such as the clergy and trade union leaders, who have special influence on public opinion. There were moral arguments, based on moral objections to a secondary principle that condoned the death penalty as a legal punishment in a civilised society, and also moral objections to a penalty for which there could be no compensation should it be discovered, subsequently, that a mistake has been made. There were also partly empirical arguments based on appeal to statistics made in countries where the death penalty had been abolished, which indicated that murders had not become more common after abolition. However, it must be stressed that the argument against the penalty as an immoral punishment in itself is independent of other arguments in that *even if* the death penalty were shown to be a deterrent and *even if* it could be guaranteed that no mistake could occur, that penalty could still be condemned. As stated earlier in this chapter, we would condemn punishment by burning at the stake even if it could be shown that such a penalty, or the threat of such a penalty, would reduce crime.

CND is an outstanding example of a currently campaigning sub-group; its members have deep objections to present government policy in regard to nuclear weapons. They think that the policy is both immoral and unwise – immoral in that the horror of nuclear war is such that there can be *no* justification for making and storing nuclear weapons, and unwise, indeed crazy, in that British possession of them increases the chance of nuclear attack. Thus on moral grounds and on empirical grounds (for concern for the survival of the human race is justifiable pragmatically as well as morally) they campaign for nuclear disarmament. They would prefer to risk foreign domination (as a lesser evil) than to risk nuclear war, though in fact they believe there is little risk of such domination though considerable risk of nuclear war. A part of this sub-group are the Greenham Common women, who are especially concerned with what they regard as the immorality and stupidity of bringing cruise missiles to British bases. It happens that the present government (1986) does not agree that there is little risk of foreign domination and does not agree that the holding of nuclear weapons increases the risk of nuclear war. No sane person wants to risk nuclear war but the government view is that, in the present situation, lack of nuclear weapons would actually increase the chances of nuclear attack for an aggressor would know that there could be no retaliation.

It is very difficult to decide who is right because the empirical facts so profoundly affect the assessment, and these facts are largely unavailable. Would there be no risk if we abandoned nuclear weapons? What are the chances of there being a nuclear war if we have them, and what are the chances if we do not have them? These questions cannot be answered, and it is difficult to see how we can set about finding the answers since we cannot conduct experiments or make historical surveys. So far majority opinion in Britain supports the government view but we do not know if it is correct. CND protestors are convinced that it is not, though they have no more empirical evidence than their opponents. But they are anxious to keep the issue before the public and they regard it as a moral duty to work to change public opinion. Many of them are prepared to use civil disobedience, breaking the laws relating to trespass and to keeping the peace, in order to carry out this duty. Undoubtedly they have been successful in drawing public attention to the problem and though, by breaking some laws, they have incurred censure they have probably gained more than they have lost from the publicity. I suggest that this is largely because whatever our views on government policy, we are aware of the lack of firm evidence and we sympathise with the concern of the campaigners. It is morally right to be concerned and though we may not think that CND have the correct solution we can agree that they are right to draw attention to nuclear issues. They are right, too, because the balance of risk inherent in policies changes with changes in technology and changes in society and constant review is necessary. CND encourages review and encourages reassessment of public attitudes.

There are many other campaigns to change current laws: some people think that the freedom to smoke soft drugs, such as cannabis, should be no more restricted than the freedom to smoke tobacco; they tend to rely on appeal to empirical evidence that these drugs do no more harm, perhaps less harm, than does tobacco and hence, they argue, it is morally wrong to make the sale of them illegal; they hope that the facts will lead to a change in public attitudes and social values. The diverse attitudes to the treatment of animals was referred to in chapter VIII; there are many aspects of this issue. Some people think that it is immoral to rear animals in order to eat them. Vegetarians may support their moral view by appealing to the fact that animal food is uneconomic and that people in Third

World countries could be adequately fed if more cereals were grown and animal husbandry were abandoned, but the moral reason for their view is the opposition to killing animals for their flesh. If their campaign succeeds and more and more people come to believe that eating animal flesh is immoral it may be that it will eventually be viewed with the same, or very nearly the same, disgust as is cannibalism.

Like some of the supporters of CND, some of these campaigners have broken the law, but the fact that they hope and expect that their protests (legal and illegal) will be effective is evidence that they believe that the community at large is a moral community and that, when it is persuaded, new social values will be established and new laws will be introduced. As John Rawls says, 'We have to recognize . . . that justifiable civil disobedience is normally a reasonable and effective form of dissent only in a society regulated to some considerable degree by a sense of justice.'[19] The word 'justifiable' begs the question, for in most disputes – protests by those opposed to laboratory experiments on animals, or protests by trade union members against laws relating to strikes, and protests against the action of some foreign power (outside an embassy), for example – one party will think that civil disobedience is justified and the other will not.[20] Moreover, as we all know, protests may go beyond civil disobedience to violence against property and persons. Sometimes this is an unfortunate development arising when tempers are high, and regretted by the organisers; sometimes it is the result of infiltration by ruffians who welcome the opportunity to create chaos. But sometimes it is the result of deliberate policy – a policy that the campaigners think is necessary because they do not think they can achieve their aims without it; if they are sincere they will *believe* that the violence is morally justified. I suspect that those animal rights campaigners who break into laboratories and attack the homes of animal research scientists believe this. They have ceased to trust the moral sense of the society in which they live. Rawls calls such people militants:

> The militant . . . is much more deeply opposed to the existing
> . . . system. He does not accept it as one which is nearly just or
> reasonably so; he believes that it departs widely from its
> professed principles or that it pursues a mistaken conception of
> justice altogether. While his action is conscientious in its own

136

terms, he does not appeal to the sense of justice of the majority (or those having effective political power), since he thinks that their sense of justice is erroneous, or else without effect . . . the militant may try to evade the penalty, since he is not prepared to accept the legal consequences of his violation of the law; this would not only be to play into the hands of the forces that he believes cannot be trusted, but also to express a recognition of the legitimacy of the constitution to which he is opposed.[21]

I doubt whether violent protestors (militants) in England today would question *in toto* the legitimacy of the parliamentary system but it is possible that at least some of them do appreciate that their actions tend to undermine more than the laws to which they overtly object. It has become fashionable among certain sub-groups to sneer at the notion of law and order for, in their view, this notion is linked very closely to that of a repressive government maintaining what order is deemed fitting to protect the status and property of the well-to-do. As we saw in chapter III, there is an inevitable tendency for words to become value-loaded, and a term such as 'law and order' can indicate a state of society in which laws are obeyed because people are contented and because they believe that the laws are just – justice is done and is seen to be done. However to militants 'law and order' carries connotations of conformity to arbitrary or biased rules imposed by a harsh, or at best obedient, police on what is, in the main, a docile or subdued populace. Most of the citizens are thought to be drilled or conditioned to accept the status quo so that order is achieved by a combination of bullying and brainwashing – the latter achieved with the help of the media. Characteristically this attitude to law and order is accompanied by the belief that the laws, and the forces of law, support a corrupt and unjust social system (see above), but this does not have to be the case. As stated above, anarchists oppose 'law and order' *in toto* because they do not think that any coercion is justified; they sincerely believe that people can live together and that daily business can be carried on smoothly and agreeably without the need for laws – rules, yes, but sanctions, no. However, most of those who profess contempt fo 'law and order' are not anarchists and despite what they assert, they do not want to abandon laws and sanctions altogether. They want new laws and a police force sympathetic to these new laws. Thus they seek to *replace* current laws to do with employment, with tenancies, with currency restrictions, finance and business, by other laws which will reflect the social values of a different social system.

We need to consider this kind of opposition to our present laws, and to their enforcement, for it is, at bottom, an opposition to our present social system, and we should reflect on whether that opposition is justified. There is no doubt that there are, and there have been, societies where maintenance of law and order has been imposed arbitrarily and that force has sustained an uncritical conformity and acceptance of the status quo: in Nazi Germany, in Tsarist Russia, in present-day Russia, and in Chile. If we wish to overthrow the British system we must believe that the injustices of that system are so great, and its laws so perverted, that it is better to incur complete disruption than to continue. There are many reasons for plotting a violent overthrow, a desire for personal glory and power being a strong one, but the only *moral* reason is based on the sincere belief that only by this means can gross injustices be removed. History tells us that revolution inevitably brings misery to many innocent people but this does not mean that no revolution is justified. The French revolution of 1789, our own Civil War in the seventeenth century, and the American colonial rebellion in 1776 may all be considered to have been justified; and hence it may be a correct moral decision to work for revolution. It is worth noting that even in the course of a revolutionary reign of terror, there can be at least lip service paid to the notion of the law as being the source of justice. For example, in his account of the Jacobin control of the French revolution in 1792, Henry Sidgwick tells us that a legal constitution was established and that it was thought that wholesale killing must be justified as legal punishment and was therefore to be preceded by some semblance of a trial, and an official sentence. He says:

At this time there were some twenty-five hundred persons in the various prisons, most of them improvised from former abbeys. . . . The cries for vengeance rang louder. Danton . . . believed that Sovereign People should set the seal of blood between them and the old *régime*; and Marat . . . made preparations. On September 2, in the Abbaye Saint-Germain, the non-juring priests were massacred, patriots of the neighbourhood acting as gentlemen executioners. But it was thought better to have the

138

business official, and a popular tribunal was appointed. The prisoners were hauled in, condemned, hauled out, and slaughtered like pigs, while the patriotic executioners shouted, '*Vive la Patrie!*'[22]

Though there may be a moral case for total disruption, and the removal of a corrupt and despotic government by revolution and bloodshed, it is difficult to find moral justification for a revolution that is aimed at changing just one particular policy, even if the government is thought to be unsympathetic and unjust. The current situation (1986) in Northern Ireland does not admit of any clear-cut practical solution because, quite apart from a host of technical problems, there seems to be no course of action that will command general agreement as being the morally right and fair course to take. Moral difficulties are much less easy to resolve than practical and technical difficulties – there is less scope for compromise. The present policy is not working but what policy would work?[23] Only one thing is certain, that revolutionary violence can do nothing but make matters worse. The same conclusion might be reached in regard to revolutionary attempts to solve religious problems in India.

As stated above, revolution is certain to bring misery to many innocent people, and complex problems cannot be solved by violence. At best violent action will bring temporary order because the 'solution' wanted by one party will be imposed on the other(s); but violence is much more likely to exacerbate the problems and increase the general suffering as well. I said above that there may be a moral case for total disruption to remove a corrupt and despotic government and bring about fundamental changes in the social system, but this can only be justified in situations where there is no alternative. However unjust we may think a society is and however much fundamental social changes are morally desirable, there can be no moral justification for violence if another course of action is available. In a parliamentary democracy there is an alternative – an alternative that has the merit of ensuring that discussion as to the desirability of the change will be possible and will take place. This is the situation in late-twentieth-century Britain and there can be no moral justification for violent political action here.

Nevertheless we have a duty, as well as a right, to make moral evaluations of our laws and to criticise those laws that we think should be changed. Moreover if legal protest fails then civil disobedience may be justified. Rawls suggests that such disobedience may actually increase social stability:

. . . civil disobedience used with due restraint and sound judgement helps to maintain and strengthen just institutions. By resisting injustice within the limits of fidelity to law, it serves to inhibit departures from justice and to correct them when they occur. A general disposition to engage in justified civil disobedience introduces stability into a well-ordered society, or one that is nearly just.[24]

By 'fidelity to law' Rawls means that those who protest through civil disobedience have a basic respect for the law, as it operates in their society. In this respect they differ from militants (see quote 21 above). Rawls develops his view:

The final court of appeal is not the court, nor the executive, nor the legislature, but the electorate as a whole. The civilly disobedient appeal in a special way to this body. There is no danger of anarchy so long as there is sufficient working agreement in citizens' conceptions of justice and the conditions of resorting to civil disobedience are respected. . . . There is no way to avoid entirely the danger of divisive strife, any more than one can rule out the possibility of profound scientific controversy.[25]

To summarise: campaigns to persuade others to change their social values are to be welcomed and non-violent infringement of laws can be justified even by those who consider that a particular protest involving civil disobedience is misguided. But in a democracy violent protest, however sincere, can have no moral justification. Such protest must, in its very nature, harm people and will almost certainly harm many people who are in no way responsible for the putative injustice that occasions the protest. It is very difficult to find moral support for violent action even in a despotic state, for the argument justifying it must rest on the assumption that good ends can justify bad means. This, as we shall see in chapter XIII, is highly dubious. It would be a dubious argument even if revolutions invariably improved society and, since they do not, the pragmatic justification is also weak.

XII

MORALITY AND RIGHTS

As we have seen, laws are made for the smooth running of society by enforcing social obligations with threat of punishment for non-compliance. Just because laws do require that obligations shall be fulfilled they help to preserve the rights of individual members of society. For the fact that, as members of a human society, we have duties and obligations towards our fellows entails that they have rights; also since others have duties and obligations towards us it follows that we too have rights. It is *logically* necessary that one who has duties confers rights on another or others. Duties are a necessary and sufficient condition for rights just as creditors are a necessary and sufficient condition for debtors. In chapter VIII I argued further than anyone who has a right must also have an obligation. This is not a logical entailment for it would be possible for a society to contain one individual who had rights (and to whom, therefore others had obligations) but who herself had no obligations to anyone. Such a person would be an autocrat, accountable to no one. However since we are concerned with moral rights, it is justifiable to take the view that no individual (with the exceptions granted in chapter VIII, note 6) can expect to have rights without also being prepared to accept obligations.

This view of rights is also to be contrasted with the view of rights as legal rules, which may or may not be moral (see chapter VIII, note 12). The moral view of rights entails that rights, though dependent on social codes, are validated by appeal to moral principles – ultimately the principle of keeping trust, but also, and more directly, the secondary principles it supports. To have a right is to be *entitled* (morally and perhaps also legally) to expect certain

141

behaviour from others; the expectations and the rights will be based on the codes of conduct accepted by society. This view of rights and duties is discussed by Finnis; he considers the Roman *jus* and shows that it had overtones of duty as well as of right:

> In Roman legal thought, '*jus*' frequently signifies the assignment made as between parties of justice according to law; and one party's 'part' in such an assignment might be a burden, not a benefit – let alone a power of liberty of choice.
>
> And in this, the vocabulary of Roman law resembles more than one pre-modern legal vocabulary. Anthropologists studying certain African tribal regimes of law have found that in the indigenous language the English terms 'a right' and 'duty' are usually covered by a single word, derived from the verbal form normally translated as 'ought'. This single word . . . is thus found to be best translated as 'due'; for 'due' looks both ways along a juridical relationship, both to what one is due to do, and to what is due to one.
>
> . . . when we come to explain the requirements of justice . . . then we find that there is reason for treating the concept of duty, obligation or requirement as having a more strategic explanatory role than the concept of rights.[1]

Then what are *natural* rights? A natural right is generally thought to be a right to have certain goods and services, and also a certain amount of freedom of expression and action along with protection of one's person, family and property. 'The rights of man' is a phrase that is differently interpreted at different times, but if these rights were really *natural* rights they would be independent of social circumstances and customs; they would depend solely on the common humanness of all people at all places and at all times. Are there such rights?

The suggestion that human beings have natural rights has greatly concerned philosophers, social reformers and humanists in the past three hundred years, that is since the time it started to be appreciated that the poor and the weak ought (morally) to have their interests considered *as of right* and not solely as a matter of benevolence. Today, in late-twentieth-century Britain, we would defend the view that the interests of any individual ought (morally) to count for as much as the interests of any other individual. This is an ideal, even though it is rarely realised in practice, and it might be seen as the basis for a code of natural rights, essentially a code of justice. Such a code would be directly related to the principle of keeping trust, and indeed must be related to a primary principle if it is to embody a 'natural' right. For natural rights are rights that we have *as human beings* and hence they must depend on a principle that is acknowledged by all (moral) human beings. A code of 'equal concern for interests' would rule that all persons had a right to expect and get fair treatment regardless of their wealth, social standing and power. I suggest that this is as far as we can go with the notion of 'natural' rights, and the outline given shows that it is rather misleading to call even this right a *natural right*. It is misleading because the idea that all persons are entitled to equal considera-tion is relatively new; in a primitive, more 'natural' society, the interests of the strongest would have been accorded much more consideration than those of others.

Claims that everyone has a natural right to food, shelter, freedom of speech, etc. are confused. For rights must arise as a result of the obligations of others, *other people*, and therefore they can only exist in a social setting where there are other people. The basic (and only) natural right – the right to equality of consideration of interests – is derived from what *today* we would call 'natural justice', and it is supported by the principle of keeping trust. But, as indicated above, the social code of any society establishes other rights that depend on the social structure. As Finnis says:

> The fact is that human rights can only be securely enjoyed in certain sorts of milieu – a context or framework of mutual respect and trust and common understanding, an environment which is physically healthy and in which the weak can go about without fear of the whims of the strong. . . .
> Just what such a milieu concretely amounts to and requires for its maintenance is something that is a matter for discussion and decision. . . . But that this is an aspect of the common good, and fit matter for laws which limit the boundless exercise of certain rights, can hardly be doubted by anyone who attends to the facts of human psychology as they bear on the realization of basic human goods.[2]

Thus in our society a child has a 'right' to receive nourishment, shelter and protection from its parents because, as we saw in chapter VII, in our society, and in the majority of human societies, it is accepted that parents have a duty to provide for their children. In our society anyone who is starving has a right to food and this is because we think that one of the duties of the state is to care for the destitute.

Hence, as well as the natural right to equality of consideration of interests, there are, in any society, social rights – rights that arise from the codes of conduct supported by secondary moral principles and social values. Some, like the duty of parents, are very firmly based and almost universally acknowledged, that is why they get confused with natural rights, but because social rights depend on secondary principles they do not have the absolute force of the natural right. However, social rights need to be distinguished from less basic rights still – legal rights. A legal right is one that is formally established by laws, but, indirectly we must hope that it will be supported by social values and by secondary moral principles. In theory then all legal rights are social rights, but, because the law is not always a reflection of social values there are occasions when a legal right conflicts with a social right, and then the law will seem to be silly or immoral. For example, at present a man is legally responsible for any debts incurred by his wife, and a creditor has a legal right to demand that a husband pay for expenses incurred by his wife. The legal right was established when women were not thought fit to own and manage property and money. Today we take a different attitude but the law has not yet altered; hence we think that in this respect the law is 'an ass' – it is silly and unjust to require a husband to pay. In addition there are some social rights that are not legal rights. For example, in our own society we feel that if someone is promised something she has a right to expect that promise to be fulfilled; but there are many occasions when important and solemn promises are broken and there can be no *legal* redress. The interdependence of natural, social and legal rights can make the question of rights seem highly complicated. In the letter below the writer is commenting on the first court ruling, condemning the *way* the government had handled the question of trade union membership for staff at the security base GCHQ at Cheltenham. The writer argues that legal rights ought (morally) to be in accord with natural justice and should establish the principle of fair treatment regardless of status. Thus the law should, in his opinion, be dependent directly on the primary moral principle of keeping trust and not on secondary principles and social values:

From Mr William Shepherd

Sir, The decision of the Court of Appeal (report, August 7) to uphold the Government's action in connexion with GCHQ Cheltenham will, I feel, give rise to concern on grounds other than those dealt with in your leader. I would add only one comment to the criticism in your leader, and that is that it was almost improper for the court to express the view that even had the Government approached the unions it would not have been of much use.

The court is in no position to form this judgment; it is not required of the court and such comment adds an unnecessary dimension to what is admittedly an extremely delicate and difficult area.

What concerns me more is the damage that is done by this decision to the concept of natural justice. This concept has been built up by judgments in the courts, particularly over the past few decades. Under it, employees of large concerns, victims of unions, professional footballers, and many others have obtained relief because of failure to carry out procedures consistent either with rules or with the broad concept of natural justice.

The Government failed miserably to carry out its moral obligations in the case of GCHQ Cheltenham and thus did immense damage to a concept that has taken some time to build up.

The nation is facing unions of increasing ruthlessness and disregard for human and national interests, looking upon any law that does not serve their sectional interest as being unfit for the statute book.

In politics the nation has become the victim of extremists on both sides. In these circumstances the preservation of the idea of natural justice assumes ever-increasing importance. It is a pity that the Court of Appeal, which is often sensitive to public feelings and needs, chose to ignore this.

Yours sincerely,
WILLIAM SHEPHERD.
77 George Street,
Portman Square, W1.
August 7.[3]

Now to assert that the law should uphold natural justice is, in one sense, redundant for if the law upholds secondary moral principles (and social values) it ought (non-morally) to uphold a primary principle, for secondary principles are derived from one of the two primary principles. If we try to make a direct connection between the law and the primary principle of keeping trust we must, of necessity, make laws that are very vaguely worded (see also chapter X) and then the application of these laws in concrete situations will depend largely on the view taken by the judge, i.e. on an individual's interpretation of natural justice. In complicated matters there will be scope for different opinions and, though there will be reasons for supporting any sincere decision, it is generally thought that a clear code is, in the long run, *more* just. Hence it is arguable that the law will serve rights better if it is justified by secondary principles.

To summarise: there is what may perhaps a little misleadingly be called 'a natural right' to justice, that is to fair treatment independent of wealth and social status. There are also social rights, some of which are enforceable as legal rights, and some of which are so well-established that they are commonly regarded as natural rights. Lastly there are some legal rights that are anomalous in that they undermine acknowledged social rights.

By relating rights to moral principles and social values we can clear away a considerable amount of ambiguity and confusion. It is now obvious that rights can only exist within society because they are a *result* of obligations between people,[4] not a cause of such obligations. A solitary human being, if one could be found, would not have a *right* to anything, but if two or more people live together, a family unit for instance, there will be obligations and therefore rights. A primitive group will not necessarily acknowledge the simple 'natural' right of equal consideration of the interests of all its members but it is likely to have quite an elaborate code of social duties and social rights.

The notion of rights has been related to theories of the origin of human societies but some of the early philosophers believed that people decided to give up their 'natural' rights when they become members of a social group. This is analogous to undertaking to behave in a certain way (and therefore giving up the 'right' to behave otherwise) when one joins a club. We can now see that the analogy is false and that such a view of rights is incoherent and a result of a misunderstanding of the term 'rights'. A person on her own can, of course, behave in any way she pleases – it is not a question of rights, it depends only on what is physically possible. As a member of a group she cannot behave precisely as she pleases, but this does not mean that she has abandoned any rights; far from it, for she had no rights to abandon. By becoming (or being) a member of a society an individual incurs obligations and acquires rights.

Thomas Hobbes (1588–1679) was a philosopher who thought that 'natural' rights were overridden when people came together to live in social groups. He said that human beings had agreed to conform to certain social rules, and to incur certain duties in order to take advantage of the protection afforded by communal living.[5] They thereby entered into a social contract. Thus Hobbes was suggesting that natural rights were curtailed by social duties and that people were prepared to suffer restrictions for they would be worse off living alone; in a solitary state their lives were nasty, brutish and short. But, from the argument above, we can see that to say that people give up rights for the sake of security is misleading; it would be clearer to say that they incur duties for the sake of security. It is also misleading to say that people *decided* to live in social groups and to imply that the social contract was formally drawn up. Hobbes, of course, lived long before there was any hint that human beings had evolved from ape-like ancestors and were in fact just another kind of animal. Nevertheless a suggestion that human groups were created by formal decision was obviously absurd even in the seventeenth century. Hobbes did not intend his contemporaries to think there had actually been a formal contract; what he wanted to stress was that human societies were to some extent artifical constructions, i.e. their codes of behaviour, their 'laws', were not 'natural' laws. The same point was to be made in the eighteenth century by Bentham. Speaking of Bentham's ideas of laws, Hart says:

> The most fundamental of these ideas is that law, good or bad, is a man-made artefact which men create and add to the world by the exercise of their will: not something which they discover through the exercise of their reason to be already in the world.[6]

But though laws were not 'natural', Hobbes, unlike Bentham, held that the authority of the law, as enforced by the state's sovereign, was not to be questioned.

Therefore Hobbes was saying that current social rights were the only ones that counted, and that legal rights, explicitly supported and enforced by the state, were the only important rights. Now we do not accept this today; we think that laws and social values must always be subject to reassessment against the primary principles. However, Hobbes's views may be interpreted so as to be considerably less unacceptable than may appear from the account so far. Firstly, if by 'natural rights' Hobbes meant just plain selfishness, to do as one pleases without considering others, then we can agree that this has to be abandoned, or much modified, in society; in that case the state as guardian of laws would be concerned to curb the 'right' to be selfish and inconsiderate. Secondly, as we shall see, Hobbes would have maintained that any law, even a bad and unjust law, was better than lawlessness; the state can give individuals so much protection that even a despotic government is better than no government. Of course Hobbes did not foresee the horrors of modern state bureaucracy or the tyranny so bitterly satirised in George Orwell's *1984*; rather his conception of the state was of a Tudor/Stuart-type monarchy; a sovereign and his advisers. The sovereign would have absolute power save that he would be restricted by the contract that required him to preserve order and traditional customs. Richard Peters writes of Hobbes's state, his Leviathan:

> The King was regarded as being limited by the 'fundamental law' embodied in the customs of the realm which guaranteed common-law rights to his subjects; similarly the sphere of his 'prerogative' was limited by tradition. But these were ill-defined as under all forms of traditional authority; there were endless controversies about cases like ship-money and monopolies which were on the border-line between the rights of the subject and the sphere of the King's prerogative. The Declaration of Rights of 1689 was an attempt to tidy up these flexible traditions on a solid legal-rational basis. The social contract theory was the theoretical justification of such concrete endeavours to end the spell of tradition; it was symptomatic of a new conception of authority which was compatible with the growing demands for liberty and equality.[7]

Yet at the end of the day Hobbes's social contract was made as a matter of expediency; it was simply more practical (not necessarily morally better) to live in a state with fixed rules and to insist that all should abide by the rules, be they good or bad. For if the rules were bad (impracticable and/or discriminatory and unfair) they were still a great deal better for the *working* of society than no rules at all. Today very few people would agree with Hobbes's view of the state as a Leviathan imposing rules that were not to be questioned; even those who do not think that there are fundamental moral principles would hesitate to justify rights that were supported by codes validated *solely* by efficiency.

A different view of the role of government was taken by John Locke (1632–1704). As we saw in chapter VI, he thought that trust was of fundamental importance and he believed that government should have a moral basis. He also believed that human rights were better preserved in society than they would be in a state of nature. Again this is to regard the imposition of duties as a withdrawal of rights rather than as a necessary condition for rights. However this is less incoherent than Rousseau's position: Jean Jacques Rousseau (1712–1788) believed that the state of nature, without organised society, had been a state of bliss; the very opposite of Locke and of Hobbes. In the state of nature men could enjoy their natural rights and any government was certain to limit those rights. One suspects that Rousseau regarded the state of nature as a state of bliss because there would be no obligations but it is very naive to assume that such a state would be one of bliss, and Rousseau's claim that man is born free and yet is everywhere in chains is suspect. Even in his own time it should have been clear that human beings had always lived in social groups and that there was no 'state of nature' because humans would always have been subject to restrictions on freedom. It is true that in the eighteenth century many governments were oppressive, but one surmises that Hobbes was probably closer to the truth in his opinion that any government would be better than none. In addition Rousseau's assertion that *man* is born free meant literally that; Rousseau's campaign for freedom from oppression and liberty was confined entirely to the rights of the male sex. As Mary Midgley has pointed out, Rousseau thought of women as utterly subservient; there was no question that they should have rights or freedom:

> Rousseau demanded unchainment. Whatever else may be
> obscure here, we tend to think that we also know who he is
> talking about – namely, all human beings. We must turn to

Émile . . . to discover that he means less than half of them;
  'Girls should early be accustomed to restraint, because all
  their life long they will have to submit to the strictest and most
  enduring restraints, those of propriety. . . . They have, or
  ought to have, little freedom. . . . As a woman's conduct is
  controlled by public opinion, so is her religion ruled by
  authority.. . . . Unable to judge for themselves, they should
  accept the judgement of father and husband as that of the
  church.'
So much for liberty; what about equality? Are women, for
instance, equally entitled to education? Rousseau replies that
they must get only the minimum which will make them useful
housekeepers and not intolerably boring housemates. Theorists
demanding more than this do not realise the fearful danger
involved. . . .
  Many things contributed to Rousseau's attitude, among them
no doubt the resentment of patronage. But it did not flow from
ignorance of other possibilities. He was being deliberately
reactionary – resisting proposals which in general his whole
basic philosophy demanded, yet which he found intolerable. He
managed his resistance by simply retreating, when this topic
came up, to the older, hierarchical style of thought which he was
busy demolishing, and using a corner of it as refuge.[8]

Theories of rights that are grounded in the purpose of human
societies do not presuppose that rights existed before society, and
hence there is less emphasis on natural rights and more appeal to
moral principles. Thomas Paine (1737–1809) took the view that the
purpose of human societies was to protect individuals (which was
Hobbes's view), and this included the right to be free (this was not
so near to Hobbes). He saw that the social systems of the countries
of northern Europe were grossly unjust and that the majority of
people had duties but very few rights and precious little liberty. He
defined liberty as being allowed to do anything that did not harm
anyone else, and although this definition can be criticised it does
give a working start to the development of ideas about freedom
within society and the function of the law. Paine's views about rights
were adopted by the Founding Fathers of the American revolution,
and their Declaration of Independence maintains that 'the pursuit
of happiness' is a right for every person and one that the state must

defend and protect. This is in accord with utilitarian morality as expounded by Jeremy Bentham (see chapter V), albeit Bentham himself demurred from discussing or advocating natural rights, thinking that the doctrine of natural rights was self-contradictory nonsense.[9]

Indeed it is. For does the question 'What is the *right* to happiness?' have a satisfactory answer? And what should the role of the state be? It may be argued that the state might aim to keep the unhappiness resulting from material deprivation at a minimum, but then we have to decide what material deprivation consists of. But *happiness* is certainly not a natural right, though it may well be a natural aspiration. In chapter VI I suggested that happiness was not necessarily the sole and certainly not necessarily the ultimate aim of human life, and that moral systems that base ultimate evaluations on happiness are suspect; but there can be no doubt that happiness is an important human aspiration. Yet does it make sense to assert that we have a *right* to happiness – even a social right? Do we have a right to good health, to successful marriage, to good fortune? All these things are desirable but are they due to each and every one of us as a matter of right?

Herbert Spencer (1820–1903) argued that the principal natural right was the right of the individual to develop her own personality and that if the state failed to allow this development then it could be defied. But what is meant by this 'development of personality' which the state is to allow? We may think that the state should enforce and regulate a social system that seeks to ensure that citizens enjoy peace, protection, food, shelter, medical care and education, yet these are but minima for the development of personality. Do we want more than this? Probably not, for most of us would *not* wish for more state direction over individual lives. Today the state has far more control over how we manage our affairs than it did in Spencer's time; there is no longer such grinding poverty and possibly there is no longer so much self-reliance. To justify yet more state supervision and control in order that there be greater opportunity for the development of personality seems ridiculous because the method would, in itself, impede the purpose. Even if we take Spencer's claim for the development of personality as a claim for social rights, we do not conclude that the state should do anything more than provide adequate material conditions and opportunities. Just how much the state ought (morally) to direct and supervise the lives of its citizens is a matter for debate but few would agree that the state, in effect the officers employed by the state (civil servants and local government officials) should be the arbiters of what 'development of personality' is, and should decide how to promote it. At the very most, and even this is doubtful, the state might play a negative role in preventing the development of personality from being hindered.

Sir Karl Popper makes the same point in regard to a possible state promotion of happiness:

> The politician . . . may or may not hope that mankind will one day realize an ideal state, and achieve happiness and perfection on earth. But he will be aware that perfection, if at all attainable, is far distant, and that every generation of men, and therefore also the living, have a claim; perhaps not so much a claim to be made happy, for there are no institutional means of making a man happy, but a claim not to be made unhappy, where it can be avoided. . . . The piecemeal engineer will, accordingly, adopt the method of searching for, and fighting against, the greatest and most urgent evils of society, rather than searching for, and fighting for, its greatest ultimate good. This difference is far from being merely verbal. In fact, it is most important. It is the difference between a reasonable method of improving the lot of man, and a method which, if really tried, may easily lead to an intolerable increase in human suffering.[10]

Any theory of social rights has to be grounded on certain contingent facts about the society concerned as well as recognising the social values, the secondary moral principles and the primary moral principles that influence what the various members of that society regard as just and reasonable. In our society, late-twentieth-century Britain, we take as social rights the right to live without fear of interference from others (including officers of the state), the right to express our ideas freely,[11] religious toleration, unbiased treatment in law and in legal disputes, fair reward for services rendered, freedom to buy and own property, freedom to spend or to save what we have earned or gained by 'lawful luck'[12] and also the right to be rescued from abject poverty. These are seen as fundamental social rights which support further rights: rights to accommodation, to medical care, to education. What more do we, or should we, expect *as of right*? For example, have we a *right* to expect congenial work?

Has an employer a *right* to dismiss an employee?

Clearly rights may conflict; certain freedoms (see note 5) must be restricted because everyone has the same rights and hence there are duties of not harming others which will limit each person's freedom. Freedom to spend our money is limited because we must insure ourselves and our fellows against misfortune; freedom to buy a house is restricted by consideration of the rights of others to buy and also by the rights of others to enjoy parks and gardens. The right to spend money is also restricted not just because some things, such as drugs, are not to be bought legally, but because some goods and services are in short supply; if the commodity is important then we judge that there is moral justification for restricting each individual's freedom and for controlling what anyone may buy. It is to be noted that control has to be justified; any restriction, whether a general restriction or one on certain persons, needs a moral justification.

Let us consider the right to spend money as we wish, money that we have acquired lawfully. Take the example of going to the theatre, a popular production that many people wish to see. Everyone has the right to buy tickets but those who book first and those who are willing and able to buy expensive seats are the only ones able to exercise their right; others are disappointed. It would be thought to be a gross infringement of the rights of the lucky few if they were later deprived of their reservation on the ground that it was unfair that they applied early or that they were able and willing to pay more. Now it might seem that exactly the same kind of reasoning can be applied to the distribution of other goods and services: medical care, housing and education; the circumstances are a little different in that there is some scope for increasing the supply, but at the end of the day there is a limit to what is available. Unlike the situation with theatre tickets, however, we do not think that those who 'come early' or who have more money should be able to indulge their right with no regard for others. We think today that there is a moral justification for restricting the rights of some, the lucky and the early birds, in order to have a fairer distribution of certain important goods and services. Arguments are about *just how much* the rights of the fortunate should be restricted.

Obviously the value of the right to act as one wishes must always be balanced against the necessity to protect others; in any society some rights have to be restricted. We have to make rules that are generally applicable, rules that allow for the importance of each and every individual's wishes and the interests of society that are incompatible with individual interests. This is not at all easy to do for, as we have seen, a very small change in circumstances can profoundly affect moral evaluation. In addition we usually have to make an evaluation without full knowledge of the relevant facts so that we must judge on the basis of guessing the consequences of any restrictions we may introduce.

Consider an even more fundamental right than the rights society gives us to education and to medical care: the right to be protected and to live in peace without fear of molestation. Now if we transgress and break society's laws we risk losing this right. It is not lost as a penalty for *any* transgression: if I park in the wrong place the police have no right to enter my house but if I have murdered someone, or am suspected of having done so, they do. Now do they have a right to violate *my* right to privacy and enter my house if I am suspected of defrauding the Inland Revenue? A court ruling a few years ago was that suspicion of such an offence did *not* give tax officers the right of forcible entry even if accompanied by the police. It was thought to be more important that people should regard their homes as inviolate than that tax evasions should be detected.

It is notorious that there are deep differences of opinion on these matters and the differences arise as a consequence partly of different assessment of the empirical facts and partly as a result of different moral assessments. It is difficult, perhaps impossible, to get agreement on the facts because this involves not only details of the relevant circumstances and consequences but also decisions as to what the relevant circumstances are, and calculations as to what the future consequences will, or might, be. Yet even if some measure of agreement be found the moral issues remain: there may be actual or potential conflict between duty and benevolence (see chapter IX) and different opinions as to the relative importance of various secondary principles and social values. Some people give more weight to benevolence than to duty; others may wish to keep certain kinds of behaviour as acts of charity not morally (and *a fortiori* not legally) obligatory. Clearly all views will be influenced by the current social values: there is no doubt that much of what would have been regarded as pure benevolence a century ago is now held to be part of social duty. But some would wish to extend social duties, others to maintain them and others to restrict them; there is an inevitable element of subjectivity, therefore, in any judgment on social issues.

However, in any society, but particularly in a large and complex society, the notion of obligation and duty is formalised in laws and accepted modes of conduct. Any list of rights (legal and moral rights) can be interpreted as a list of social obligations: the right to live in peace entails obligations not to harm or to interfere with others; the right to express our ideas freely entails the obligation to tolerate others expressing their ideas. To acknowledge that rights must entail obligations may not in itself solve social problems but it may help to solve them; for it may be helpful to treat conflicts of rights as conflicts of obligations – by so doing we become more aware of another point of view.

When we make assertions about social values we have certain moral principles, secondary moral principles, in mind; they provide the ground of obligations and rights that we deem to be desirable. Thus we may assert that goods and services *ought* to be evenly distributed and we may wish to justify greater equality of distribution. We shall probably believe that one political system offers the best means for obtaining the kind of society that we think is (morally) best. But whatever party we support, and whatever means we think ought (pragmatically) to be adopted to attain the best society, they must, if we are concerned with morality, be compatible with our basic moral principles. Thus however great are our moral ends, they cannot justify behaviour that entails malevolence (torture, physical and mental) or behaviour that entails betrayal of trust and injustice. There can be no moral justification of means that flout the basic moral principles, however morally desirable are the ends in view. And, as a matter of practical morality, experience shows that immoral means do *not* result in the attainment of moral ends, for the means corrupt the ends.[13] At the end of chapter XI I said that *violent* illegal actions could not be justified in a democratic society; but illegal actions could sometimes be justified. We must bear in mind that illegal actions are not necessarily immoral and certainly do not necessarily flout the *basic* moral principles. It may be necessary to use force within society (the legal sanctions or the force of revolution) and between societies (war), but gratuitous harm to others and betrayal of trust cannot be morally justified. To claim, for instance, that the bombing of Hiroshima was morally justified because it prevented the deaths of

155

many more Allied (and Japanese) soldiers and civilians is to engage in moral equivocation. Quite apart from the fact that we cannot be even reasonably sure that a bomb dropped on a rock near to Japan would not have led to capitulation, we must insist that some actions are absolutely wrong and cannot have a moral justification.

Any immoral action tends to degrade and corrupt the agent; thus it becomes progressively easier to be immoral, and there is increasing readiness to accept specious arguments, particularly arguments that rely on justification of means by appeals to ends. It is part of the danger of many moral theories and political creeds – utilitarianism, communism and various forms of religious evangelicalism – that the end, some ultimate good, is thought to justify immoral means for its achievement. It is part of the danger of what Stuart Hampshire has called 'rational computational morality':

> There is a presumed distinction between rationality in choosing between lines of conduct, practical reason, and rationality in arriving at true statements and beliefs, theoretical reason,[14] and this distinction is associated with a specific account of practical reasoning . . . the word 'rational', as it occurs in the phrase 'rational computational morality', can be part of a reproach, because of the implication that the wrong model of rationality is involved; wrong in the sense that it is inappropriate to reasoning of other kinds.[15]

Hampshire wishes to stress that the kind of reasoning used in logic and mathematics, and in assessing matters of empirical fact, is just not appropriate when assessing moral behaviour, i.e. making value judgments. Certain actions just *ought not* to be and no amount of emphasis on the desirability of the ends they may bring about should persuade us to tolerate them.

Even Hart, who inclines to utilitarianism and rational justifications, is concerned to find a theory of rights that can be a satisfactory successor to utilitarianism:

> . . . it is plain that a theory of rights is urgently called for. During the last half century man's inhumanity to man has been such that the most basic and elementary freedoms and protections have been denied to innumerable men and women guilty, if of anything, only of claiming such freedoms and protections for themselves and others, and sometimes these

have been denied to them on the specious pretence that this denial is demanded by the general welfare of a society. . . . I cannot here assess how much or how little the world has gained from the fact that in the thirty years which separate the signing of the United Nations Charter from the recent Helsinki Agreement, pressure for the implementation of basic human rights has become increasingly a feature of international relations, conventions, and diplomacy. Nor can I assess here how often cynical lip service to the doctrine has been, and still is, accompanied by cynical disregard of its principles. There is however no doubt that the conception of basic human rights has deeply affected the style of diplomacy, the morality and the political ideology of our time, even though thousands of innocent pesons still imprisoned or oppressed have not yet felt its benefits. The doctrine of human rights has at least temporarily replaced the doctrine of maximising utilitarianism as the prime philosophical inspiration of political and social reform. It remains to be seen whether it will have as much success as utilitarianism once had in changing the practices of governments for human good.[16]

If we take rights (and laws) as the embodiment of obligations and duties then we can appreciate that they are determined by our moral principles and social values. They also help to mould those principles and values; there is interdependence as with morality and the law. The problem of rights is the problem of deciding where our social obligations lie and this will depend on our social values. As Hart implies it is a problem between societies as well as within societies. Laws are implemented by the courts but they are largely the result of political decisions; they are made by politicians. We need to consider whether a special kind of behaviour ought (morally) to distinguish politicians, *qua* politicians, from other citizens.

XIII

THE MORALITY OF POLITICS AND POLITICIANS

The word 'politics' is derived from the Greek word '*polis*', a city; Aristotle defined man as a political animal, meaning a social animal, one who lived in cities. Both Plato and Aristotle thought that human beings were *essentially* social beings; they believed that the most fulfilling human life was one devoted to the welfare of fellow citizens through service to the state. In Ancient Greece it was the city state that was a self-governing and independent unit. All adult male citizens, whether rich or poor, were able to debate and influence the policies of their own city.[1]

In Plato's ideal state, described in his *Republic*, a corps of guardians, selected in early youth for their ability, were to be specially trained to devote their lives to governing the State. All children were to be reared together, not in separate homes, so that parents would not form attachments and there would be no nepotism. Thus selection for the class of guardians would be based solely on the basis of each individual's character and qualities. Not that the guardians would have an easy and luxurious life; they were to live austerely, and although they would have great power, they would also be conscious of their responsibilities and of the trust that all the citizens had in them.

Of course there is much to criticise here. How could the correct selection be made early? We now know that selection at the age of eleven or thirteen years is not satisfactory, and that is selection solely for intellectual, not moral abilities. And if it were possible to devise better methods, would it be wise to bring up children communally in institutions? It is possible that if this were the established custom parents would be prepared to part with their

158

babies, but our present knowledge of child development leads us to believe that the effect of deprivation of personal affection from parents or parent substitutes is likely to be disastrous. In any case even if highly intelligent and altruistic guardians could be selected and educated, is it likely that they would remain ascetic and altruistic when they had power? Would they not be tempted to use their position to seek self-aggrandisement, if not material luxuries, and to form a despotic oligarchy? Nepotism would surely follow and the whole system would steadily deteriorate from the Platonic ideal. There is no reason to suppose that Acton's maxim, 'Power tends to corrupt and absolute power corrupts absolutely,'[2] would not apply to Platonic guardians.

Today practically all societies pay lip service to democracy, understood as some form of representative government; any form of obligarchy, e.g. our own House of Lords, needs to be justified, the burden of proof being on those who support it. *A fortiori* any attempt to impose a single ruler is thought to bring about bad government however benevolent the ruler may seem. Past experience shows that we are right to be highly suspicious of concentration of power.

But there are grave drawbacks inherent in democratic government. Firstly, we have to accept that democracy in a modern state is very different from the democracy of a city state in Ancient Greece. Unlike the Greek citizen, citizens of today's democracy cannot vote on every matter of policy, not even on those issues thought to be especially important. Secondly, were such frequent voting possible, it is very unlikely that many people would understand the issues, their consequences and their implications. Most people would not have time to concern themselves more than superficially and, in the late twentieth century, many issues are complex and can be understood only by those who professionally concerned. Thirdly it will often be the case that people do not know what policy is in their ultimate interest and in the best interest of the community in which they live, and of mankind in general. Lastly, and this is perhaps the most important criticism, we cannot assume that even if people were aware of what policy would be in the best interest of society they would support it if it conflicted with what they considered to be their own immediate interests. 'Democracy' was originally a pejorative term, signifying 'mob rule' and therefore 'bad rule'.

John Stuart Mill, although in favour of democracy, strongly

opposed what he called 'the collective mediocrity of the masses'. But he was writing at a time when the masses were barely literate. He advocated more education, along with better social conditions in general, and he thought that the whole community would thereby become more intelligent and would use the power gained through enfranchisement wisely. Then the government, truly representative and democratic, would be wise and just. Mill was influenced by Plato and the Platonic theory that those who are educated will be wise and will appreciate that a government that promotes the general good (and not sectional or personal interests) will also promote the long-term good of each individual. It is reasonable to believe that Mill himself was genuinely altruistic but unfortunately he was exceptional. There is absolutely no evidence to show that better educated and more affluent people are more altruistic or even more politically wise than those who are less sophisticated and less comfortably placed.

It seems that human beings are always liable to be egotistical (see the beginning of chapter XI) and cannot be relied upon to support policies that conflict with their immediate interests. Moreover they seem unable to conduct public affairs even so as to further interests that are to be justified prudentially rather than morally. Barbara Tuchman, in her book *The March of Folly*, describes various examples of policies that were a result of whole series of mistakes in judgment, mistakes so bad that they can only be accounted for by assuming that judgment is corrupted by short-sighted selfishness. She says:

> Folly's appearance is independent of era or locality; it is timeless and universal, although the habits and beliefs of a particular time and place determine the form it takes. It is unrelated to type of regime: monarchy, oligarchy and democracy produce it equally. Nor is it peculiar to nation or class. The working class as represented by Communist governments functions no more rationally or effectively in power than the middle class, as has been notably demonstrated in recent history. Mao Tse-tung may be admired for many things, but the Great Leap Forward, with a steel plant in every backyard, and the Cultural Revolution were exercises in unwisdom that greatly damaged China's progress and stability. . . . The record of the Russian proletariat in power can hardly be called enlightened. . . . If the majority of

Russians are materially better off than before, the cost in cruelty and tyranny has been no less and probably greater than under the czars.[3]

We have to acknowledge that we human beings are singularly inept at managing our political affairs. The incompetence is not due to lack of intelligence but to our short-sighted selfishness which makes it very difficult for those in power to act morally and to pursue policies that they know, in their heart of hearts, are morally right, rather than policies that they think (invariably wrongly) are expedient or will help to keep them in office. It is of prime importance that those who govern be perpetually reminded of moral values; we cannot expect them to be morally perfect but we can evaluate their political actions and we need to have moral as well as pragmatic (prudential) criteria. Those who best satisfy these criteria are less likely to fall into folly.

Finally we have to consider whether the criteria for public morality are different from those we adopt for personal morality; whether the morality expected from politicians *qua* politicians must differ from their morality as private people. The latter will be the same as it is for anyone who is a member of the society, but there are different factors relevant to the moral assessment of public conduct. We may find that it is sometimes necessary for a politician to condone and even advocate actions that would be immoral[4] if she, or anyone else, acted similarly at a personal level. For example, as representing the state, a politician must condone and indeed expect the use of force in upholding the law. As Stuart Hampshire points out:

> In the normal run of things the moral problems associated with the use of force, and with war and violence, do not arise in private life. The occasional use of violence, and the normal uses of force and of threats of force, introduce their own moral conflicts.[5]

Hampshire draws our attention to the fact that the decisions of politicians are likely to affect a large number of people and so politicians have obligations and duties not only as private individuals but, in their role of politician, as representatives of many others. The consequences of their political decisions are likely to be much more far-reaching than the consequences of private activities and Hampshire goes so far as to concur with Machiavelli's implication that for the politician consequences, or ends, are so important, that they may justify means that would be immoral for a private person:

> Machievelli implied that morality in politics must be a consequentialist morality, and the 'must' here marks a moral injunction. A fastidiousness about the means employed, appropriate in personal relations, is a moral dereliction in a politician, and the relevant moral criterion for a great national enterprise is lasting success; and success is measured by a historian's yardstick; continuing power, prosperity, high national spirit, a lasting dominance of the particular state or nation in the affairs of men.[6]

This alarming conclusion is somewhat mitigated by the requirement that politicians must be more explicit as to their reasons for taking a certain line of action than must private citizens. Thus when a policy is criticised politicians can attempt to justify it by appealing to the consequences, as opposed to the consequences of adopting another policy; they do not have to rely solely on appeal to moral principles and social values. They have to say not only that their actual policy results in the best (or least bad) consequences but also how and why this is so. Even so I am reluctant to agree with Machiavelli: his view of success is itself morally dubious and it is even more morally dubious to assent to its attainment by immoral means.

Nevertheless (see note 4) it may be allowed that politicians must bear in mind factors that will affect their ranking of secondary moral principles as compared with the relative importance given to such principles by private individuals. The fundamental principles remain categorical but the application to actions and the secondary principles derived from them can vary. Thus it is not that we require an *entirely* different set of social values for politicians as politicians, but rather that in their capacity as rulers, or potential or aspiring rulers, they have particular responsibilities that require special evaluation. For though as private persons we are responsible for our actions and may be required to justify them to certain people on occasion, politicians must be publicly accountable for their political actions and decisions at all times. Though they must be prepared to relegate some private scruples based on secondary moral principles and thus be prepared to use force, they must also be prepared to explain why they do this.

In fact many people are cynical as to the morality of politicians, certainly as to their principles in relation to public affairs. It is believed that they decide to do what will be popular in order to stay in office, and that at least some of them succumb to the temptation of taking advantage of their position to make their own lives more comfortable and improve their personal finances. How politicians actually do behave has some bearing on any judgment as to how they ought to behave, because we cannot require what experience shows is not humanly possible. Any politician has a moral obligation to assess the merits of the not improper wish to stay in office; it has to be acknowledged as a factor bearing on any decision and may not be entirely due to personal ambition.

In so far as politicians use their position for *direct* personal gain they are crooked if not criminal; cases of corruption are not unknown, for politicians, like all human beings, are capable of immorality, and even of short-sighted immorality. However it is *not* requiring something beyond human powers to require that temptations to 'feather one's nest' be resisted. The fact that such conduct will bring certain disgrace contributes to making it unlikely to be common. Immorality at a *personal* level, i.e. not as a result of holding office, is probably as common among politicians as among private persons. Logically there is no more reason to censure a politician for sexual immorality or for driving offences than anyone else. The fact that her misdeed will attract more publicity in itself makes any social (including legal) punishment more severe. However a politician who shows that she has succumbed to private temptation is *perhaps* more likely to be seduced into public wrongdoing. Though one cannot establish the connection by logical argument, it is possible that morality cannot be separated into private and public components. Hence arise demands that a politician found guilty of private immorality should resign, recognising that at least to some extent she has shown her moral character *qua* politician, as well as *qua* private person, to be tarnished.

A politician's moral principles will be strained if the government of which she is a part (or the party to which she belongs) initiates (or supports) policies with which she disagrees. However, she may have good *moral* reasons not to resign. She may, for example, think she will do more good by working to correct the error (as she sees it) from within; or, that as she disagrees only on one issue, she is justified in supporting the government (or party) overall; or that, although the policy is morally wrong, it seems to be needed in order to achieve desirable ends. This (see above) shows a divergence between public and private morality. There is no doubt that, except when considering relatively straightforward public issues – such as the need to make regulations ensuring that water will not be polluted by germs, to protect children from committing themselves by contract and to impose regulations requiring drivers to insure against injuries to others – a politician will have to advocate policies that do not carry universal moral approval and which she may find morally disagreeable. Public affairs are complex and though it is an ill wind that blows nobody any good, it is also a remarkably fair wind that does nobody any harm. It may be that those with a scrupulous moral sense are not psychologically suited to be politicians; they should, perhaps, get out of the kitchen if they find it too hot, as President Truman advised.

But this could be dangerous for it may be much better to have politicians who are genuinely reluctant to carry out policies they find morally disagreeable. We *need* people who will take moral factors seriously for then they will only support morally disturbing policies if they conclude that they are absolutely necessary and will avoid them if it is feasible to do so. We do not want to be governed by those who think that ends justify means and, *a fortiori*, we do not want to be governed by those who believe that *any* means are justified if the ends in view are important. The very most we should accept is a reluctant acquiesence to the relegation of secondary moral principles and a reluctant setting aside of the social values they support.

It is for this reason that, as Hampshire says, we should not approve the suggestion that those who have to endorse severe punishments, e.g. that traitors should be shot, or those who, on balance, believe that some scientific experiments on animals are justified and therefore are not to be made illegal, should themselves do the shooting and conduct (or watch) the experiments. For our most moral politicians will be people who are disturbed at what they decide they *have* to permit and who would not be prepared to do such things themselves. If they were so prepared, or if it was understood that they were required to carry out such morally unpleasant tasks, they would be more likely to be people who were

The morality of politics and politicians

willing to give the relevant orders and to condone the laws without disquiet. Worse still, they might well come to enjoy the violence they had the power to inflict. What we want of our political system is that it should bring forward people who have a decent moral sense and who have high personal moral integrity. They have to bear morality in mind even when they are concerned with ends and therefore we hope that they will always be reluctant to abandon their principles and will always be prepared, and in fact be required, to justify their decisions.

XIV

PRACTICAL REASON: SENSE AND SENSIBILITY

In everyday life we have to make moral judgments fairly quickly, and we make use of *ad hoc* rules to guide our conduct. These rules are related to moral principles and social values but, in general, we do not think about such things, we follow the moral custom. We may think that we know intuitively what is right and what is wrong but most of our judgments are heavily influenced by social conditioning. This is inevitable and, in day-to-day affairs, it is necessary that we should have ready rules. However, it follows that if the rules are questioned, and when we have to engage in moral debate, we find deliberation difficult and perhaps disturbing. We are not accustomed to relating our rules to secondary principles, let alone deriving the latter from primary principles; and, in assessing our rules, we may have difficulty in distinguishing the moral from the conventional components. As Geoffrey Warnock says, there can be confusion about the content of morality: 'When we talk about "morals" we do not all know what we mean; what moral problems, moral principles, moral judgments are is *not* a matter so clear that it can be passed over as a simple datum.'[1]

By investigating the nature of moral judgments and the sense and scope of the word 'moral' we are in a position to assess our *ad hoc* rules; constructive criticism gives a firmer basis for moral evaluation and will almost certainly show that many so-called moral disagreements are disagreements about matters of fact. Ayer[2] was quite right to say that many purportedly moral disagreements and ethical arguments are largely about the facts of the situation, the possible consequences of action and the intentions of the agent(s), but he

166

was wrong to assert that there was no possibility of rational *moral* debate. As we have seen, different people 'weigh' moral issues differently and there can be differences of opinion as to how secondary principles relate to primary principles; these matters, although involving feeling, are subjects for rational debate. Therefore:

> Investigation of the sense and scope of 'moral' is desirable not only because it seems prudent that, in moral theory, we should decide what we are talking about. It is also possible that such investigation should show what the basis is for making moral distinctions – that is, what class or range of considerations, identifying an issue as a moral isuse, are consequentially relevant to moral assessment.[3]

Ethics help us to pick out the *moral* element in judgments and to be aware of the interdependence of fact and value. It leads us to appreciate the complexities of moral assessment and of moral evaluation. We have seen that purely moral concepts of goodness, duty and benevolence are closely related and that less purely moral words such as 'chaste' can have changing value overtones. Clearly moral judgments carry a psychological penumbra which can greatly influence our attitude and in this respect there is a difference of degree between moral judgments and logical and empirical judgments. No judgment made by human beings is entirely free of a subjective element but personal emotions influence moral judgments much more strongly than they influence other kinds of judgment. However, the unique feature of moral judgments is that they are based on consideration of the interests of those other than the agent, a consideration that I suggest is referred to the two fundamental principles: keeping trust and benevolence.

Though all human societies depend on the members keeping trust and though benevolence is in fact universally acknowledged, they can and do survive with moral free riders who, if undetected, may gain more material goodies and more status than their more moral fellows. Indeed most of us free ride from time to time for we have moral lapses: the occasional failure to fulfil obligations and the occasional act of meanness or of spite. Some people may not even feel guilty, for human beings have a remarkable power for self-deception and, as we saw in chapter III, the same action can be described in such different ways that the implicit moral evaluation is entirely different. The more honest we are with ourselves the more readily we will acknowledge our moral lapses but we do tend to minimise self-blame for, psychopaths apart, we are anxious to see ourselves as moral beings and to be so thought of by others. The question 'Why should I be moral?' is a rhetorical question, analogous to 'Why should I be human?'. Just as Thomas Carlyle (1795–1881) is supposed to have remarked 'Gad, she'd better!' about the lady who announced that she accepted the universe, we have to accept our humanity and that we are the kind of creatures that we are.

Contrast between the moral and the prudential is made by Bernard Levin. In the following extract he uses the word 'moral' to signify 'acting in one's own (admittedly enlightened) interest' and 'honourable' to mean 'acting in accord with moral principle'. He says:

> H.L. Mencken . . . drew distinction between the *honourable* man, who always keeps his promises, and the *moral* man, who keeps his promises sometimes but breaks them at other times; at the other times, he defends his breach of promise by reference to a higher morality, a greater good, the avoidance of a greater evil. Mencken, being Mencken, pointed out that these latter instances invariably coincide with what will benefit the moral man most, but it is not necessary to assume hypocrisy, likely though it is; assume that honour is honourable and morality moral, and then say which comes first?. . .
>
> The moral man's actions can never be free of ambiguity, and his appeal to a higher standard than that of a promise made, a promise kept, cannot be tested . . . every man's ladder will have removable rungs, so that they can be moved about as necessary. 'I would rather lose the election than deceive the people' is never true, but even if it were it would always be subject to a higher truth; 'I must deceive the people because otherwise the safety of the realm would be endangered'.
>
> Here are two tombstones, both with your name and date of birth on them. Be assured that when the date of your death comes to be filled in also, those in charge of the proceedings will add either 'He *always* kept his word' or 'He *always* acted from the best motives'. Which would you choose?[4]

Lord Devlin makes an analogous distinction between morality and the law, between moral behaviour and legal behaviour:

> No man is worth much who regulates his conduct with the sole
> object of escaping punishment, and every worthy society sets for
> its members standards which are above those of the law. We
> recognise the existence of such higher standards when we use
> expressions such as 'moral obligation' and 'morally bound'. The
> distinction was well put in the judgment of African elders in a
> family dispute: 'We have the power to make you divide the
> crops, for this is our law, and we will see this is done. But we
> have not the power to make you behave like an upright man.'[5]

One does not have to study ethics to appreciate the moral significance of the last two quotations any more than it was necessary
to study ethics to evaluate Falstaff's view of honour, as given at the
end of chapter I. But ethics can help us to assess our evaluations and
to have better appreciation of the content of morality. The impact
of a moral judgment is through our emotions but its long-term
strength comes from the support given by reason. Just as a study of
logic improves and refines our natural capacity for what Aristotle
called speculative reason, so ethical study improves our natural
capacity for practical reason. In this respect reason is not the slave
of the passions nor their mistress, but their coadjutant.

GLOSSARY

Analytic	An analytic truth is one that can be known to be true by consideration of the terms (by analysis); an analytic approach to a statement is a criticism based on rational analysis and is to be contrasted with an empirical approach when criticism is based on appeal to evidence and to the possibility of error.
Condition	Necessary: A necessary condition is one which must obtain if an event is to occur or a statement is to be true. For example air being present is a necessary condition for human life, and the possibility of inter-subjective agreement is a necessary condition for the statement 'This is an objective truth' to be true.
	Sufficient: A sufficient condition is one which will bring about an event if it obtains. For example if a person's head is cut off she will die so that decapitation is a sufficient condition for death.
Consequent	The latter part of a hypothetical statement, e.g. '*q*' in 'If *p* then *q*'. See also *modus ponens* and *modus tollens* below.
Contingent	Something which just happens to be the case: it is not necessarily or logically inevitable. It is a contingent fact that I am alive.
Empirical	Based on observation (sense perception).
Epistemic	Of knowledge and of the grounds for knowledge.
Epistemological	Of the theory or science of the grounds for knowledge and the methods for obtaining knowledge.
Imperatives	Categorical: A guide to action that is not conditional on anything else; thus 'keep trust' can be treated as a categorical imperative which does not need any justification.

Hypothetical: A guide to action which is justified and depends on some condition, e.g. 'Be honest', with an implied '*if* you want to keep trust'. The hypothetical imperative can be overruled, a person may steal to feed the starving and could argue that there was a greater duty of trust to do this. Mackie would argue that all moral imperatives are (ultimately) hypothetical in that they imply a reference to what the speaker wants, even if only inner self-respect.

At this point I have argued (in chapter VI) the imperative is effectively categorical; 'keep trust if you want to be moral'.

Modus ponens   A valid inference of the form 'If p then q; p; therefore q', or 'If this gas is hydrogen then it is explosive; it is hydrogen, therefore it is explosive'.

Modus tollens   A valid inference of the form 'If p then q; not q; therefore not p' or 'If this gas is hydrogen then it is explosive; it is not explosive, therefore it is not hydrogen'.

In both types of inference the antecedent in the first premise is 'This gas is hydrogen' and the consequent is 'It is explosive'.

Normative   Ethical statements or moral judgments which imply rules for behaviour rather than description of social conventions or laws.

Ontological   Of existence and of the manner of existence.

Ostensive definition   Definition by pointing; thus if someone asked 'What is a horse?', I might point to one as an example. Certain things must be ostensively defined, e.g. 'What does "red" mean?'

Platonic forms   For Plato any general term like 'horse', 'justice' or 'holiness' was a real though non-material entity. Indeed the Forms (also called Ideas and Universals) were ultimate reality and what we could perceive with our senses were mere shadows. We could come to know the Forms by mental contemplation.

Tautology, tautologous   A repetition, either direct – 'A rose is a rose' – or saying the same thing in a different way, e.g. 'A quadruped is four-footed'. If we say that a person is wise if and only if she is good, then to follow this by 'The wise are good' is tautologous; the statement is a tautology in that context.

Telos   Purpose.

Truth   Coherence theory: A statement is true if it is consistent with all other statements that are accepted as true.

Utilitarianism

Correspondence theory: A statement is true if it *corresponds to* what is the case.

An ethical theory which serves to provide a criterion, that of utility (happiness), whereby actions could be morally evaluted. For Jeremy Bentham the principle of utility was for the evaluation of laws; he was not concerned with personal morality. John Stuart Mill developed utilitarianism to apply to individuals' actions and the moral evaluation of people's behaviour.

NOTES AND REFERENCES

CHAPTER I   MORALITY DOES MATTER

1   Jennifer Trusted, *Free Will and Responsibility*, Oxford University Press, 1984.
2   Ibid., Preface and chapter 21.
3   David D. Raphael, *Moral Philosophy*, Oxford University Press, 1981, p.9.
4   John Finnis, *Natural Law and Natural Rights*, Oxford, Clarendon Press, 1980, p. 12.
5   The Greek word '*arete*' is translated as 'virtue', but 'virtue' did not have the same meaning for the Ancient Greeks as it does for us. Our concept of virtue is based on our Christian as well as our Greek heritage. This influences us whether or not we are Christians. For the Greeks, '*arete*' could not stand on its own, as 'virtue' can for us; for them to have *arete* was to have it in respect of something. They would speak of a 'governing *arete*' (good at governing) and of a 'military *arete*' (good at warfare)' and so on. They would speak of a dog or horse having *arete* – that is being a good dog or horse. Likewise a person having *arete* was good at being a human being.
6   Aristotle, *Ethics*, trans. J.A.K. Thomson, revised Hugh Tredennick, 1st edn, 1953; Harmondsworth, Penguin, 1976, p.63.
7   The Biblical account of the Fall gives rise to two main problems: firstly, if God was all-powerful why were Adam and Eve allowed to eat the fruit and lose their innocence; secondly, how, without knowledge of good and evil, was it possible for the pair to be capable of sin? In their state of innocence they were amoral creatures and could no more be blamed than the animals. In his essay 'The Heroic Poem in a Scientific Age', Basil Willey, *The Seventeenth Century Background*, Chatto & Windus, London, 1934, pp. 205–263, discusses Milton's treatment of these problems in *Paradise Lost*. I have considered Milton's approach to the problem of freedom elsewhere (op. cit., Trusted, pp. 25–7). According to Willey, Milton attempted to solve the problem of moral

guilt by arguing that Adam and Eve did know that it was wrong to disobey God and eat the fruit; also the tree did not confer special moral knowledge. It was the disobedience, not the fruit, that brought about the Fall, for 'Adam *learnt* nothing from the tree, he merely fell into the fate of "knowing good and evil", that is, of experiencing sin and misery and contrasting them with past innocence' (ibid., p.257).

8 See also chapter VI, quote 2.
9 Richard Whately, Archbishop of Dublin, Apopthegm, *Oxford Dictionary of Quotations*, Oxford University Press, 1959, p.565.
10 William Shakespeare, *Henry IV, Part I*, Act V, Sc.i.
11 The cynic may contend that though few would endorse Falstaff in public, more than a few would act on his words. However, this is to concede the point that we appreciate Shakespeare's satire on a moral trimmer. At least Falstaff is not a hypocrite, he refuses to pay the customary tribute (hypocrisy) that vice pays to virtue; but he *is* immoral, and we all know this.

CHAPTER II   JUDGMENTS

1 Judgments may also be called 'statements' or 'propositions'.
2 The distinction is not so sharp as is implied here, but it is appropriate to maintain it here.
3 Eugene Ionescu, *Plays*, vol.I, trans. Donald Watson, London, John Calder, 1958, pp. 16–18.
4 It is possible to produce plausible alternative solutions in advanced mathematics (see chapter X).
5 P.H. Nowell-Smith, *Ethics*, Oxford, Blackwell, 1957, p.46.
6 Ibid., pp. 47–8.
7 The justification of stipulative definition of a 'real' property is given by A.J. Ayer in *The Central Questions of Philosophy*, London, Weidenfeld & Nicholson, 1973, pp. 78–9.
8 I am not concerned with some ultimate metaphysical reality, but with objective empirical facts as opposed to subjective experiences.
9 Touching, or holding hands near to an object. Judgments of temperature can also be made on the basis of colour and change of size. But no consistently reliable method of temperature measurement was possible before the invention of the mercury thermometer and the standardising of scale by reference to two fixed points.
10 Because we can get agreement among observers with normal sense perception, *who are also qualified to interpret what is observed*. The latter proviso applies to observations made with sophisticated instruments.
11 Again it is assumed that those judging are adequately qualified.
12 Nowell-Smith, op. cit., p.49.

13 Thomas Kuhn and Paul Feyerabend, for example. See also reference to Willard V.O. Quine in chapter VI.

14 Many philosophers of science, e.g. Sir Karl Popper, do not think that any scientific theory can be known to be true, but they do think that we are justified in taking science to be a quest for objective truth. 'Truth' is in accord with human experience, not a metaphysical concept.

15 John Finnis, *Natural Law and Natural Rights*, Oxford, Clarendon Press, 1980, p.32.

16 Ibid., pp. 67–8.

17 Ibid., p.385.

18 It would seem that this is intuitive and not the result of social conditioning since all human beings in all societies structure their world in this way. There is some evidence that animals also do so.

19 Of course the vast majority of people assume that space is Euclidean without having any knowledge or understanding of Euclid and the axioms.

20 Finnis, op. cit., p.70.

21 Jennifer Trusted, *Free Will and Responsibility*, Oxford University Press, 1984, chapters 11 and 12.

CHAPTER III   FACT AND VALUE

1 As is shown later, there are circumstances in which we decide that we are not under a moral obligation to keep trust, but in general betrayal of trust invites moral censure.

2 We should note that the fact that most people think that it is desirable to protect doctors and priests and probably not desirable to protect journalists does not entail that protection (or lack of protection) is better (pragmatically) or better (morally). The argument for or against such protection is generally pragmatic and a moral argument, though it may be supported by a pragmatic argument, does not depend on it. Those who believe that a trust is sacred will keep faith whether or no they are protected by the law.

3 It would be thought wrong to burn people for any reason, of course, but we need not deal with the general issue here. See also chapter XI.

4 I am not concerned with the metaphorical use of these words.

5 If spoken the tone of voice can communicate moral evaluation.

6 D. Young, letter to *The Times*, 15 September 1982.

7 Some philosophers consider that the method of measuring a quality *is* the source of the definition of that quality.

8 We can avoid subjectivity by defining intelligence as that which is measured by intelligence tests (see note 7 above), but then we have kept the bath water and thrown out the baby.

9 At the boundary of each subject there will be regions of conjecture and dispute about the explanations offered. But the 'core' of each subject

consists of an accepted body of theories, well supported by empirical facts. These theories are not immune to refutation but in practice they are taken as firm ground for the science.

10 There can be general agreement as to what the price *is*, even when there is no agreement as to what the price *ought* to be. Take, for example, arguments about the price that butter from the European 'butter mountain' was sold for to the Russians.

11 Oscar Wilde, *Lady Windermere's Fan*, Act III.

12 Proverbs, 31, verse 10.

CHAPTER IV   EMOTIVISM AND PRESCRIPTIVISM

1 A.J. Ayer, *Language, Truth and Logic*, London, Gollancz, 1970, p.107.

2 Ibid., pp. 109–10.

3 Ludwig Wittengenstein, 'A Lecture on Ethics', *Philosophical Review*, 1965, pp. 11–12.

4 Ayer, op. cit., p.108.

5 Donald Hudson, *Modern Moral Philosophy*, London, Macmillan, 1970, p.157.

6 Geoffrey J. Warnock, *Contemporary Moral Philosophy*, London, Macmillan, 1974, p.45.

7 Richard Hare, *Freedom and Reason*, Oxford, Clarendon Press, 1963, pp. 147–8.

8 Ibid., pp. 155–6.

9 Ibid., p.88.

10 Ibid., pp. 89–90.

CHAPTER V   CONSEQUENTIALISM: HAPPINESS AND JUSTICE

1 J.S. Mill, *Utilitarianism*, ed. Mary Warnock, London, Collins/Fontana, 1978, p.254.

2 Ibid., p.257.

3 Ibid., p.258.

4 Ibid., pp. 259–60.

5 Ibid., p.261.

6 Ibid., p.268.

7 Ibid., p.269.

8 Ibid., p.263.

9   Ibid., p.267.
10 Aldous Huxley, *Brave New World*, London, Folio Society, 1971, chapter 1, pp.16–17.
11 Ibid., chapter 5, pp.58–9.
12 John Finnis, *Natural Law and Natural Rights*, Oxford, Clarendon Press, 1980, pp.95–6.
13 J.S. Mill, 'On Liberty', from *Essential Works of John Stuart Mill*, ed. Max Lerner, London, Bantam Books, 1965.
14 Ibid., p.307.
15 John Gray, *Mill on Liberty: A Defence*, London, Routledge & Kegan Paul, 1983, pp.125–6.
16 Ibid., p.127.
17 Anthony O'Hear, *Experience, Explanation and Faith*, London, Routledge & Kegan Paul, 1984, p.205.
18 Ibid., p.211.
19 P.H. Nowell-Smith, *Ethics*, Oxford, Blackwell, 1957, p.194.
20 Stuart Hampshire, 'Morality and Pessimism', from *Public and Private Morality*, ed. Stuart Hampshire, Cambridge University Press, 1980, p.1.
21 Ibid., p.3.
22 Ibid., p.4.
23 Isaiah Berlin, 'Equality', from *Concepts and Categories*, London, Hogarth Press, 1978, p.96.
24 Hampshire, op. cit., p.16.
25 Ibid., p.18.
26 Bernard Williams, *Morality: An Introduction to Ethics*, Cambridge University Press, 1976, p.65.
27 Ibid., p.108.
28 Anthony Quinton, *Utilitarian Ethics*, London, Macmillan, 1973, p.45.
29 Ibid., pp.61–62.
30 Ibid., p.63.
31 Mill, *Utilitarianism*, pp.288–9.
32 Quinton, op. cit., p.70.
33 Ibid., p.71.
34 Ibid., p.79.
35 John Rawls, *A Theory of Justice*, Oxford University Press, 1980, pp.141–2.
36 Ibid., p.488.
37 Thomas Nagel, 'Moral Luck', from *Free Will*, ed. Gary Watson, Oxford University Press, 1982, p.179.
38 Ibid., p.180.
39 Nagel draws our attention to a paradox in that our sense of fairness requires us not to blame a person for events beyond her control and yet in fact moral judgments are made in the light of what happens. In *Mind*, no.378, April 1986, pp.198–209, Norvin Richards seeks to resolve the paradox by suggesting that the moral judgment is based on character and disposition and that what happens is important only in so far as it provides evidence of character.

CHAPTER VI   INTUITIONISM

1   Leviticus, chapter 19, verse 18, and St Matthew, chapter 19, verse 19.
2   Patrick Devlin, 'Morals and the Criminal Law', reprinted in *The Philosophy of Law*, ed. Ronald Dworkin, 1977, p.69.
3   H.J. Paton, *The Moral Law*, London, Hutchinson, 1976, p.67.
4   Ibid., p.91.
5   Ibid., p.72.
6   Ibid., p.114.
7   Ibid., pp.114–15.
8   G.E. Moore, *Principia Ethica*, Cambridge University Press, 1903, reprint 1922, p.x.
9   Ibid., p.18.
10 Ibid., pp.8–9.
11 Ibid., p.14.
12 Samuel Clarke, 'On Natural Religion', *British Moralists*, vol. II, ed. Selby-Bigge, New York, Bobbs-Merrill, 1964, p.6.
13 Ibid., p.13.
14 The fundamental importance of trust was recognised by John Locke in the seventeenth century. See John Dunn, *Locke*, Oxford University Press, 1984, p.52.
15 John L. Austin, *Sense and Sensibilia*, Oxford, Clarendon Press, 1962, pp.70–71.
16 See also chapter XI.
17 Anthony O'Hear, *Experience, Explanation and Faith*, London, Routledge and Kegan Paul, 1984, p.82.
18 'Superhuman telos' means 'superhuman, or divine, purpose'.
19 O'Hear, op. cit., p.83.
20 Quoted by Antony Flew, *An Introduction to Western Philosophy*, London, Thames & Hudson, London, 1971, pp.27–8.
21 Peter Singer, *The Expanding Circle*, Oxford University Press, 1983, p.9.
22 John L. Mackie, *Ethics*, Harmondsworth, Penguin, 1977, pp.77–8.
23 This is not to debase morality to prudence (see chapter I); rather, as is shown in the next quotation, it is to say that prudence can be elevated to morality.
24 Mackie, op. cit., p.190.
25 Ibid., pp.191–2.
26 John Keats, 'Ode on a Grecian Urn'.
27 Quoted by Christopher Hassall in *Edward Marsh*, London, Longman, 1959, p.510.
28 Ibid.,pp.510–11.
29 Eric R. Dodds, *The Greeks and the Irrational*, Cambridge University Press, 1951, p.31.
30 Ibid., p.18.
31 William Shakespeare, *Hamlet*, Act III, Sc. iii.
32 Willard V.O. Quine. 'On the Nature of Moral Values', *Theories and*

Things, Cambridge, Mass., The Belknap Press of Harvard University Press, 1981, p.62.

33 John Finnis, *Natural Law and Natural Rights*, Oxford, Clarendon Press, Oxford, 1980, p.83.

34 Quine, op. cit., p.63.

35 W.V.O. Quine, 'Responses', in *Theories and Things*, op. cit., p.181.

CHAPTER VII   CONVENTIONS OF TRUST AND INSTITUTIONAL FACTS

1 There are a few societies, such as the Israeli kibbutz, where parental care is not expected, but there is a moral duty of care owed to children by adults.

2 Richard Lovelace, 'To Lucasta, Going to the Wars'.

3 William Shakespeare, *Macbeth*, Act I, Sc. vii.

4 Richard Wagner, *Die Walkürie*, Act I, Sc.ii, libretto, trans. William Mann, 1972, published for EMI Records. I am indebted to Mr Nicholas Gale of Exmouth for reminding me of this example of the obligation of a host to his guest.

5 J.R. Searle, 'How to Derive "Ought" from "Is" ', *Philosophical Review*, no. 73, 1964.

6 John L. Mackie, *Ethics*, Harmondsworth, Penguin 1977, p.71.

7 Homosexuals are more restricted than heterosexuals; for example the age of consent for heterosexuals is sixteen years whereas for homosexuals it is twenty-one years, but the restrictions are, like this one, at least of the same kind.

8 An obligation to a third person may be rendered theoretical by the availability of effective contraceptives; the fact that these are available has itself affected moral codes of sexual behaviour; see also chapter XI.

CHAPTER VIII   BENEVOLENCE: MAN AND BEAST

1 A. Ross, letter to *The Times*, 4 September 1984.

2 1 Corinthians, chapter 13, verses 1–6.

3 William Shakespeare, *The Merchant of Venice*, Act IV, Sc. i.

4 See the letter to *The Times*, quoted in chapter III, note 6.

5 We may wish to remove hardship without thinking that the best interests of individuals are served by satisfying all wants. See chapter V and quotations from *Brave New World*.

6 We must except children, the mentally defective and the senile. These

people do not have obligations (or very few) and therefore are not *complete* persons. We allow them rights either because they will become persons or because they were or might have been persons and it would be very difficult, perhaps impossible, to have distinct categories of human beings only some of whom had rights.

7 Christopher Hibbert, *Africa Explored*, London, Allen Lane, 1982, pp.30–1.

8 Ibid., p.36.

9 Mary Webb, *Precious Bane*, book 3, chapter 1, London, Virago, 1978, pp.145–8.

10 See also chapter VI, p.69.

11 Thomas Henry Huxley, 'On the Hypothesis that Animals are Automata, and its History', quoted by Godfrey Vesey in *Body and Mind*, London, Allen & Unwin, 1964, pp.138–9.

12 Obviously children have rights (see also note 6 above), and many people consider that a foetus has rights. Like the mentally ill, the mentally defective and the senile, they are restricted in their rights; they do not have the rights of ordinary adults. Full rights are accorded only to those who have obligations. I would suggest that for this reason the 'rights' that a master has over his slaves in a slave-owning society are dubious unless that master acknowledges certain duties. His rights are much less than the rights of a parent over a child or even an employer over an employee.

It is to be stressed that we are concerned with moral rights, not legal rights. As Professor Hart makes clear (H.A.L. Hart, 'Positivism and the Separation of Law and Morals', in Ronald Dworkin's *The Philosophy of Law* (Oxford University Press, 1977, pp. 21–2), a *rule* that confers rights need not be a moral rule. (Note that Hart's essay is in a different form from that in his book *Essays in Jurisprudence*, Oxford, Clarendon Press, 1983.)

13 Following Peter Singer's line, I am taking *person* to mean 'rational and self-conscious being' and accepting the view that we should at least entertain the notion that some species of non-human animals should be acknowledged as persons. See Peter Singer, *Practical Ethics*, Cambridge University Press, 1979, pp.91–6.

14 *The Times*, 2 December 1982.

CHAPTER IX   MORAL CONFLICT AND RATIONAL CHOICE

1 A.J. Ayer, *Language, Truth and Logic*, London, Gollancz, 1970, p.110.

2 Ibid., p.111.

3 If we do not accept the validity of *modus ponens* for instance, we can become involved in an infinite regress of inference. See Lewis Carroll,

'What the Tortoise said to Achilles', *Mind*, New Series no.15, July 1895, pp.278–80.

4   Jonathan Dancy, 'Ethical Relativism and Morally Relevant Properties', *Mind*, vol. 92, 368, October 1983, pp.530–47.

5   Ibid., p.534.

6   Ibid., p.546.

7   Ibid.

8   Stuart Hampshire, 'Public and Private Morality', in *Public and Private Morality*, Cambridge University Press, 1978, p.31.

9   Jean-Paul Sartre, *Existentialism and Humanism*, trans. Philip Mairet, London, Eyre Methuen, 1973, pp.35–6.

10   Of course we do not *necessarily* think another's choice to be morally right and I am not suggesting that all moral choice can be morally justified. It can only be through acknowledgment of a rational relationship to the basic moral principles that we can give moral approval to any decision or action. What I am suggesting is that there are circumstances when it is morally defensible and rational for there to be different moral choices.

11   Aristotle, *Ethics*, trans, J.A.K. Thomson, revised Hugh Tredennick, Harmondsworth, Penguin, 1976, pp.123–4.

12   Ibid., p.122.

13   Sartre, op. cit., pp 49–50.

14   Ibid., p.54.

CHAPTER X   SECONDARY PRINCIPLES AND SOCIAL VALUES

1   Some of the differences in social values within societies are discussed in this chapter, others were referred to in chapter VIII. Societies of many millions of people will inevitably be composed of sub-groups holding at least some different social values. See also chapter VII.

2   Today a pregnant woman incurs less risk through clinical abortion than if she comes to term and has the baby.

3   Peter Singer, *Practical Ethics*, Cambridge University Press, 1979, p.122.

4   Michael Lockwood (ed.), *Moral Dilemmas in Modern Medicine*, Oxford University Press, 1985, chapter 1.

5   In the nineteenth century it was thought that working-class people should not drink because they would not be able to fulfil their obligations to their families and to society, but there was no corresponding censure of those who were more prosperous.

6   There are prudential reasons as well of course; as in so many other fields, the moral and the prudential are not clearly distinguishable.

7   We are in process of change and probably the majority of people think that sexual fidelity in marriage is highly desirable. But it is no longer

grounds for divorce. In the nineteenth century one infidelity was adequate grounds for a husband to divorce his wife; a wife had to show that her husband was persistently unfaithful.

8   Jonathan Lear, *Mind*, no. 365, January 1983, pp.40–60.
9   At first Lear contrasts this with the possibility of giving a coherent picture of a tribe with a different morality from our own (different secondary principles) but he concludes finally that apparently different moral outlooks may be converging. This is a rejection of moral relativism and, by implication, acceptance of the view that different human societies have fundamental moral principles in common.
10 For everyday purposes Euclidean geometry does mirror the world.
11 Lear, op. cit., p.48.
12 The Cantorian account of infinity entails that an infinite set is characterised by containing the same number of entities in any sub-set as are in the whole set. Thus there are as many even numbers as there are numbers in the infinite set of real numbers; likewise as many cubes as real numbers, and so on. It follows that there are the same number of years in infinity plus eighty as there are in an infinite number of years.
13 Lear, op. cit., pp.49–50.
14 Of course methods of disposal of the dead can have moral overtones because customs and rites valued by living relatives and friends may be followed or flouted. The story of Antigone and Creon illustrates this aspect, but, important as this is, it does not bear on the argument here.
15 This is not logical necessity; it arises from the way human beings happen to structure their world. It does have a conceptual necessity. See also chapter V on the concept of a person.

CHAPTER XI   MORALITY AND THE LAW

1   H.L.A. Hart, 'Positivism, Law and Morals', p.50. *Essays in Jurisprudence and Philosophy*, Oxford, Clarendon Press, 1983, p.50.
2   John Austin, 'The Province of Jurisprudence Determined', Lecture 2, from *Utilitarianism*, ed. Mary Warnock, London, Collins/Fontana, 1962, p.33.
3   Hart, op. cit., p.52.
4   Ibid., p.55.
5   Convicted criminals may admit that they acted wrongly on particular occasions. Alternatively they may plead extenuating circumstances as justification. But, psychopaths apart, they firmly resist imputations of total immorality.
6   The somewhat unpleasantly sanctimonious censure that ordinary criminals indulge in when discussing crimes of rape, child abuse and brutal attacks shows their wish to be accorded respect as moral agents.

By showing their disapproval of greater crimes, lesser criminals seek to establish that they do have moral principles.

7   Lord Devlin, 'Morals and the Criminal Law', from *The Philosophy of Law*, ed. Ronald Dworkin, Oxford University Press, 1977, pp.71–2.

8   Ibid., pp.76–7.

9   Ibid., p.78.

10 Ibid., p.81.

11 H.L.A. Hart, 'Immorality and Treason', from Dworkin, op. cit., p.85.

12 Ibid., p.87.

13 There are said to be witches' covens in England today and perhaps some of their activities are illegal: but whatever they do no one seriously believes that they have the powers attributed to witches in medieval times.

14 H.L.A. Hart, 'Social Solidarity and the Enforcement of Morality', in *Essays in Jurisprudence*, see note 1.

15 Even, in some cases, insisting on the terms of a contract, though the law is complicated here. The case of Shylock is so well known that the demand for 'a pound of flesh' is a way of describing such insistence. However Shylock's terms would be unenforceable in Britain today so that no Portia would be needed to defend Antonio.

16 C.E.M. Joad, *Guide to the Philosophy of Morals and Politics*, London, Gollancz, 1938.

17 Any one person may be a member of several sub-groups, each with characteristic codes. For example a person might be a member of the Conservative party, a trade unionist and a vegetarian; another might be a Roman Catholic, a member of the SDP and a member of the National Trust. As long as codes do not directly conflict any one person can be a member of very diverse sub-groups.

18 We are not concerned with the ordinary criminal who breaks the law for entirely selfish reasons, but with those who break the law because they think that the law is wrong or that another law, to which they wish to draw attention, is morally wrong.

19 John Rawls, *A Theory of Justice*, Oxford University Press, 1972, p.387.

20 The moral justification of protest is discussed not only by Rawls, ibid., but also by Peter Singer in *Democracy and Disobedience*, Oxford University Press, 1973.

21 Rawls, op. cit., p.367.

22 Henry Dwight Sidgwick, *A Short History of France*, London, Harrap, 1934, p.278.

23 This is not intended to imply that British rule in Northern Ireland *is* despotic. Certain sub-groups, in particular the IRA, think that it is, but even if they were right, this would not justify violence.

24 Rawls, op. cit., p.383.

25 Ibid., p.390.

CHAPTER XII   MORALITY AND RIGHTS

1   John Finnis, *Natural Law and Natural Rights*, Oxford, Clarendon Press, 1980, pp.209–10.
2   Ibid., p.216–17.
3   William Shepherd, letter to *The Times*, 9 August 1984.
4   As explained in chapter VIII, it seems less confusing not to regard animals as having rights. We shall favour kindness (benevolence) to animals and condemn malevolence but, since animals cannot have obligations at any stage in their lives, they are not the kind of creatures to have rights.
5   According to Professor Hart the same kind of view is expressed by Nozick:

> Thus Nozick argues that, granted a set of natural rights, such as not to be killed, assaulted, or coerced, and not to have property taken or destroyed and not to be limited in the use of property, only a minimal form of State . . . can be legitimate. Moreover given these natural rights even this minimum form of State could be justified only under conditions . . . conditions produced out of Nozick's lively imagination which are highly unlikely to be satisfied in the real as contrasted with the imaginary world. The conditions in question are that the State should have arisen through individuals voluntarily joining a private association which might eventually achieve, if without infringing any natural rights, dominance in a limited territory even if not everyone joined. (H.L.A. Hart, 'Law in the Perspective of Philosophy', from *Essays in Jurisprudence*, Oxford University Press, 1983, p.151)

6   H.L.A. Hart, op. cit., p.146.
7   Richard Peters, *Hobbes*, London, Penguin, 1967, p.187.
8   Mary Midgley, 'Sex and Personal Identity', *Encounter*, June 1984, p.52.
9   Hart, op. cit., p.181.
10   Karl Popper, *The Open Society and its Enemies*, London, Routledge & Kegan Paul, 5th edn 1966, p.158.
11   There are restrictions on these and other freedoms because other members of society have the same rights. This is discussed later in the chapter.
12   'Lawful luck' is good fortune through, for example, inheritance, gifts, and from various forms of gambling.
13   See also below, p.156.
14   Hampshire adopts Aristotle's (translated) terminology – see chapter I – and uses the terms 'practical reason' and 'theoretical reason' to signify moral and empirical reasoning respectively.
15   Stuart Hampshire (ed.) 'Public and Private Morality', *Public and Private Morality*, Cambridge University Press, 1978, p.23.
16   Hart, op. cit., pp.196–7.

CHAPTER XIII THE MORALITY OF POLITICS AND POLITICIANS

1 We have to bear in mind that Ancient Greek societies were slave-owning societies and that the slaves had no say in government.
2 Sir J.E.E. Dalberg, first Baron Acton, letter in *Life of Mandell Creighton*, 1904, vol. 1, quoted in *The Oxford Dictionary of Quotations*, Oxford University Press, 1959, p.1.
3 Barbara Tuchman, *The March of Folly*, London, Michael Joseph, 1984, p.6.
4 Politicians frequently have to disregard or relegate secondary moral principles and social values, but there are, in my view, no circumstances that can justify abandoning the primary principles unless there is a conflict at that level. See chapter IX and the end of chapter XII.
5 Stuart Hampshire (ed.), 'Public and Private Morality', *Public and Private Morality*, Cambridge University Press 1978, p.49.
6 Op. cit., p.50.

CHAPTER XIV PRACTICAL REASON: SENSE AND SENSIBILITY

1 Geoffrey Warnock, *Contemporary Moral Philosophy*, London, Macmillan, 1967, p.75.
2 See chapter IV, p. 28 and A.J. Ayer, *Language, Truth and Logic*, London, Gollancz, 1970, pp.110–11.
3 Warnock, op. cit., p.75.
4 Bernard Levin, 'How to give away $3 and be able to live with yourself', *The Times*, 24 August 1984, p.8.
5 Lord Devlin, 'Morals and the Criminal Law', from *The Philosophy of Law*, ed. Ronald Dworkin, Oxford University Press, 1977, p.82.

FURTHER READING

Many of the books listed in the notes provide useful reading, and the notes themselves indicate the relevance of the various books to particular topics. The suggestions made here include many of those titles and others which have not been directly referred to or quoted from in the main text.

There are many good general books on ethics. A good and recent introduction to the subject is D.D. Raphael's *Modern Moral Philosophy* (Oxford University Press, 1981), and another less recent but very readable book is A.C. Ewing's *Ethics* (London, English Universities Press, 1953). A more detailed survey is given by W.D. Hudson in *Modern Moral Philosophy* (London, Macmillan, 1970); this favours the prescriptivist view of moral judgments. In his short and very informative *Contemporary Moral Philosophy* (London, Macmillan, 1967) Geoffrey Warnock inclines to a consequentialist justification of moral judgments, evaluations being according to the promotion of human welfare. In Chapter 6 of his *Language Truth and Logic* (London, Gollancz, 1970) A.J. Ayer gives a spirited account of the emotivist position. Richard Hare's *The Language of Morals* (Oxford University Press, 1952) and *Freedom and Reason* (Oxford University Press, 1963), develop the prescriptivist view that originated with Hare. The intuitionist view as formulated by Immanuel Kant in *The Moral Law*, trans. H.J. Paton (London, Hutchinson, 1948) is still well worth reading. Other writers favouring various intuitionist analyses of moral judgments are George E. Moore in *Principia Ethica* (Cambridge University Press, 1953), a modern classic, also H.A. Prichard in *Moral Obligation: Essays and Lectures* (Oxford University Press, 1949), W.D. Ross in *The Right and the Good*, (Oxford, Clarendon Press, 1961) and C.D. Broad's *Five Types of Ethical Theory* (London, Kegan Paul, Trench & Trubner, 1934).

The best introduction to utilitarianism is still John Stuart Mill's essay 'Utilitarianism'; this is in many collections of Mill's works including *Utilitarianism*, ed. Mary Warnock (London, Collins/Fontana, 1962). The utilitarian view is developed and defended by Anthony Quinton in his *Utilitarian Ethics* (London, Macmillan, 1973) and a modified utilitarianism is advocated by Peter Singer in his *Practical Ethics* (Cambridge University Press, 1979). He is concerned with treatment of animals and this is discussed by Mary Midgley in *Animals and Why They Matter* (Harmondsworth, Penguin 1983).

Utilitarianism is criticised by Bernard Williams in his *Morality: An Introduction to Ethics* (Cambridge University Press, 1976) and by G.R. Grice in *The Grounds of Moral Judgment* (Cambridge University Press, 1967). Both these books require some prior reading, as does P.H. Nowell-Smith's *Ethics* (Oxford, Blackwell, 1957) – this book has final chapters on freedom and responsibility. Kant had stressed that morality presupposed freedom and I make the same point in my own *Free Will and Responsibility* (Jennifer Trusted, Oxford University Press, 1984). A more sceptical view of moral principles and moral values is given by John Mackie in his *Ethics* (Harmondsworth, Penguin, 1977), an excellent short and readable account of many modern writers' views is given by Mary Warnock in *Ethics since 1900* (Oxford University Press, 3rd edn 1978).

The social nature of ethics is discussed by Peter Singer in *The Expanding Circle* (Oxford University Press, 1981) and by Elizabeth Anscombe in her *Ethics, Religion and Politics* (Oxford, Blackwell, 1981), especially in Part 3, and also in the collection of essays edited by Stuart Hampshire, *Public and Private Morality* (Cambridge University Press, 1978), which is generally anti-utilitarian. Peter Singer appeals to utilitarian criteria in his *Democracy and Disobedience* (Oxford University Press, 1973) and so do most of the contributors to the discussion of aspects of medical ethics in *Moral Dilemmas in Medicine*, ed. Michael Lockwood (Oxford University Press, 1985). Books concerned with the relation of morality to the law are *The Philosophy of Law*, ed. Ronald Dworkin (Oxford University Press, 1977), H.L.A. Hart's *Essays in Jurisprudence* (Oxford, Clarendon Press, 1983) and John Finnis's *Natural Law and Natural Rights* (Oxford, Clarendon Press, 1981). There are some essays on ethical aspects of education in *Education, Values and Mind* (ed. David Cooper London, Routledge & Kegan Paul, 1986). Two important books concerned with society and morality are Robert Nozick's *Anarchy, State and Utopia* (Oxford, Blackwell, 1974) and John Rawls's *A Theory of Justice* (Oxford University Press, 1972).

Books discussing the role of religion in morality are, again, Anscombe's *Ethics, Religion and Politics* (see above), Anthony O'Hear's *Experience, Explanation and Faith* (London, Routledge & Kegan Paul, 1984) and chapters 6 and 9 of John Mackie's *The Miracle of Theism* (Oxford, Clarendon Press, 1982). The latter two are not championing Christianity and nor is Jean-Paul Sartre's *Being and Nothingness*, translated by Hazel Barnes (New York, Philosophical Library, 1956), which is not Christian and gives a secular existentialist account of moral judgments.

Two general collections of essays for those having some familiarity with the subject are *Utilitarianism and Beyond*, eds. Amartya Sen and Bernard Williams (Cambridge University Press, 1982) and *The Is-Ought Question*, ed. W.D. Hudson (London, Macmillan, 1969).

BIBLIOGRAPHY

ARISTOTLE, *Ethics*, Harmondsworth, Penguin, 1976.

AUSTIN, J.L., *Sense and Sensibilia*, Oxford, Clarendon Press, 1962.

AYER, A.J., *Language, Truth and Logic*, London, Gollancz, 1970.

AYER, A.J., *The Central Questions of Philosophy*, London, Weidenfeld & Nicolson, 1973.

BERLIN, I., *Concepts and Categories*, London, Hogarth Press, 1978.

DODDS, E., *The Greeks and the Irrational*, Cambridge University Press, 1951.

DWORKIN, R. (ed.), *The Philosophy of Law*, Oxford University Press, 1977.

FINNIS, J., *Natural Law and Natural Rights*, Oxford University Press, 1981.

FLEW, A., *An Introduction to Western Philosophy*, London, Thames & Hudson, 1971.

GRAY, J., *Mill on Liberty: A Defence*, London, Routledge & Kegan Paul, 1983.

HAMPSHIRE, S. (ed.) *Public and Private Morality*, Cambridge University Press, 1980.

HARE, R.M., *Freedom and Reason*, Oxford, 1965.

HART, H.L.A., *Essays in Jurisprudence and Philosophy*, Oxford, Clarendon Press, 1983.

HASSALL, C., *Edward Marsh*, London, Longman, 1959.

HIBBERT, C., *Africa Explored*, London, Allen Lane, 1982.

HUDSON, W.D., *Modern Moral Philosophy*, London, Macmillan, 1970.

HUXLEY, A., *Brave New World*, London, The Folio Society, 1971.

JOAD, C.E.M., *Guide to the Philosophy of Morals and Politics*, London, Gollancz, 1938.

LOCKWOOD, M., *Moral Dilemmas in Modern Medicine*, Oxford University Press, 1985.

MACKIE, J.L. *Ethics*, Harmondsworth, Penguin, 1977.

MILL, J.S., *Essential Works*, (ed.) Lerner, M., New York, Bantam Books, 1965.

Bibliography

MILL, J.S., *Utilitarianism*, (ed.) Warnock, M., Collins/Fontana, London, 1978.

MOORE, G.E., *Principia Ethica*, Cambridge University Press, 1903.

NOWELL-SMITH, P.H., *Ethics*, Oxford, Blackwell, 1957.

NOZZICK, R., *Anarchy, State and Utopia*, Oxford, Blackwell, 1974.

O'HEAR, A., *Experience, Explanation and Faith*, London, Routledge & Kegan Paul, 1984.

PATON, H.J., *The Moral Law*, London, Hutchinson, 1976.

PETERS, R., *Hobbes*, London, Penguin, 1967.

POPPER, K., *The Open Society and its Enemies*, London, Routledge & Kegan Paul, 1966.

QUINTON, A., *Utilitarian Ethics*, London, Macmillan, 1973.

RAPHAEL, D.D., *Moral Philosophy*, Oxford University Press, 1981.

RAWLS, J., *A Theory of Justice*, Oxford University Press, 1980.

SARTRE, J.S., *Existentialism and Humanism*, trans, Mairet, P., London, Eyre Methuen, 1973.

SELBY-BIGGE, L.A. (ed.), *British Moralists*. New York, Bobbs-Merrill, 1964.

SIDGWICK, H.D., *A Short History of France*, London, Harrap, 1934.

SINGER, P., *Democracy and Disobedience*, Oxford University Press, 1973.

SINGER, P., *Practical Ethics*, Cambridge University Press, 1979.

SINGER, P., *The Expanding Circle*, Oxford University Press, 1983.

TRUSTED, J., *Free Will and Responsibility*, Oxford University Press, 1984.

TUCHMAN, B., *The March of Folly*, London, Michael Joseph, 1984.

VESEY, G. (ed.) *Body and Mind*, London, Allen & Unwin, 1964.

WARNOCK, G.J., *Contemporary Moral Philosophy*, London, Macmillan, 1974.

WARNOCK, M. (ed.), *Utilitarianism*, London, Collins/Fontana, 1962.

WATSON, G. (ed.), *Free Will*, Oxford University Press, 1982.

WEBB, M., *Precious Bane*, London, Virago, 1978.

WILLEY, B., *The Seventeenth Century Background*, London, Chatto & Windus, 1984.

WILLIAMS, B., *Morality: An Introduction to Ethics*, Cambridge University Press, 1978.

INDEX